ISBN 978-0-282-69102-8
PIBN 10861649

# 1 MONTH OF
# FREE
# READING

## at

## www.ForgottenBooks.com

By purchasing this book you are
eligible for one month membership to
ForgottenBooks.com, giving you
unlimited access to our entire
collection of over 1,000,000 titles via
our web site and mobile apps.

To claim your free month visit:

www.forgottenbooks.com/free861649

English
Français
Deutsche
Italiano
Español
Português

# www.forgottenbooks.com

**Mythology** Photography **Fiction**
Fishing Christianity **Art** Cooking
Essays Buddhism Freemasonry
Medicine **Biology** Music **Ancient
Egypt** Evolution Carpentry Physics
Dance Geology **Mathematics** Fitness
Shakespeare **Folklore** Yoga Marketing
**Confidence** Immortality Biographies
Poetry **Psychology** Witchcraft
Electronics Chemistry History **Law**
Accounting **Philosophy** Anthropology
Alchemy Drama Quantum Mechanics
Atheism Sexual Health **Ancient History**
**Entrepreneurship** Languages Sport
Paleontology Needlework Islam
**Metaphysics** Investment Archaeology
Parenting Statistics Criminology
**Motivational**

# GUIDE TO
# MUSKOKA LAKES,
## Upper Maganetawan & Inside Channel of the
# GEORGIAN BAY.

The Famous
FISHING,
HUNTING
& Pleasure
Resorts of
ONTARIO

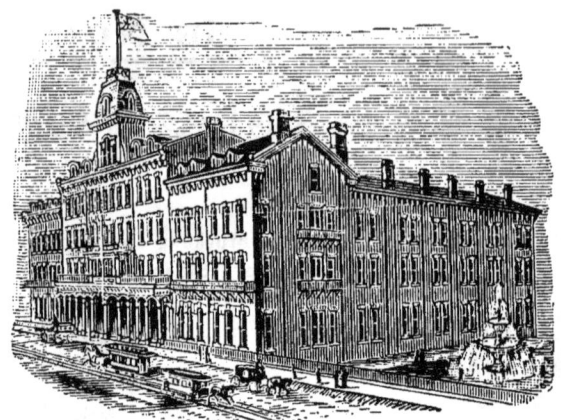

# The Queen's Hotel,

## TORONTO.

### Strictly First-class in all its Appointments.

Celebrated for its home comforts, perfect quiet, excellent attendance, and the peculiar excellence of its cuisine; it has been patronized by their Royal Highnesses Prince Leopold and the Princess Louise, the Marquis of Lorne, Lord and Lady Dufferin, the Marquis and Marchioness of Lansdowne, and the best families. Is most delightfully situated near the Bay, on Front Street, and is one of the largest and most comfortable hotels in the Dominion of Canada.

### McGAW & WINNETT, - Proprietors.

---

# QUEEN'S ROYAL HOTEL.

## NIAGARA-ON-THE-LAKE, ONT.

This Hotel and Summer Resort is located in a beautiful grove opposite Fort Niagara, at the head of Lake Ontario and the mouth of the Niagara River. It is capable of accommodating three hundred and fifty guests. All modern improvements. The drives along the banks of the Lake and River are beautiful and refreshing.

Application for rooms may be made to the proprietors of the Queen's Hotel, Toronto, up to June 1st, after that date to the "Queen's Royal," Niagara-on-the-Lake, Ont.

## McGAW & WINNETT, Proprietors.

# PREFACE.

The purpose of this little Guide Book, as may be seen from the limited space devoted to original descriptive matter, is not literary display, but rather to impart useful general information for intending visitors to the Lakes of Muskoka, to the island shores of the Georgian Bay, and to the Magnetawan. A considerable variety of descriptive matter, the experience of disinterested travellers has, however, been compiled within these pages, a perusal of which is confidently commended to the reader.

# INDEX.

**For Index to Advertisemets see page 125.**

# MUSKOKA AND GEORGIAN BAY.

## THE HIGHLANDS OF ONTARIO.

THE Muskoka Lakes and Georgian Bay may reasonably be designated *par excellence*, the desirable holiday resort of the Western Hemisphere, a comparatively new territory, yet the short experience has already demonstrated that it possesses real advantages, whether from a scenic, recuperative, or economic standpoint.

The fresh and pure air of this elevated region, with its picturesque surroundings of lake and forest, cannot fail to invigorate exhausted physical nature. The peculiar softness of the limpid water and resinous odour of the pine forests are most health giving. To the lovers of acquatics the sheltered lakes afford safe boating and fishing, and to those who prefer to rusticate on shore, delightful rambles in the woods, or a constitutional on the colonization roads can be indulged in, to say nothing of drives, and short and long excursion trips upon the numerous pleasure steamers. Farther on the reader will find descriptions of each of the three great divisions of the Muskoka and Georgian Bay resorts, with further general information and lists of hotels, guides, etc., with modes of access, cost of same, ticket agents, rates of fares, time tables, new game laws, etc., etc.

## MAGNETAWAN DIVISION.

Comprising a magnificent river and lake sail of upwards of forty miles, starting from Burk's Falls Station
on the Northern Division of the Grand Trunk Railway, passing through Magnetawan Village into Ahmic
Harbour, the foot of navigation, where connections
can be made by stages to Parry Sound, via. McKellar
and Dunchurch. Very good hotel accommodation at
Burk's Falls, and fair accommodation at all the other
places of call. Excellent speckled trout, bass and
pickerel, are found in great quantities in this region.

A novelty of the route is the excellent daily passenger and freight steamer " Wenonah," propelled by
both paddles and screw, the only craft of the kind on
the continent. The principle of combined paddles
and screw has proved to be quite a success in this
instance.

## THE COACH ROUTES AND TRIBU-
## TARY RESORTS.

The eighteen mile drive, between Port Cockburn on
Lake Joseph, and Parry Sound on Georgian Bay, is a
pretty and interesting one. The road winds its way
along hill and dale amid bright lakelets on either hand.
The journey is easily accomplished in from three to
four hours, and without fatigue. The road to Ahmic
Harbour, thirty miles, is for the most part of the same
class.

Several good fishing lakes are to be found near the
waggon road. Star lake, one of the Seguin chain, five

miles to the northward of Port Cockburn, is worthy of mention. Mr. W. F. Thomson has recently provided excellent accommodation for tourists on the shore of that lake. Otter, Horse Shoe, and White Fish Lakes, are fine sheets of water, and a little further to the south, are the famed fishing lakes, Blackstone and Crane. There are upwards of 800 lakes, linked together by foaming streams, in the Muskoka and Parry Sound regions.

## GEORGIAN BAY DIVISION.

Comprising a sail of upwards of 150 miles from Penetanguishene and Midland to French River, via. the Town of Parry Sound. The route of the steamers is through the most sheltered and picturesque portions of the great Georgian Bay archipelago.

The discovery of these new inside channels dissipated the terrors of Georgian Bay.

The first class upper cabin paddle steamer, " F. B· Maxwell," makes daily trips in close connnection with the Northern Division of the Grand Trunk Railway at Penetanguishene, and Midland, to Parry Sound over the justly famed inside route. The staunch propeller "Imperial" makes semi-weekly trips as far as Byng Inlet and French River, calling at Midland every Wednesday and Saturday, and Collingwood on Saturday afternoons, thence to Parry Sound at 11 a.m., on Mondays. These steamers have state-room accommodation for passengers, and the fishing along their route is unexcelled in fresh waters. Stage connections at Parry

Sound with the Muskoka Lakes, eighteen miles distant, and with the Upper Maganetawan at Ahmic Harbour, thirty miles distant. Excellent hotel accommodation at Parry Sound.

## THE MUSKOKA DIVISION.

Comprising the island dotted lakes, Muskoka, Rosseau and Joseph, extends a distance of fifty miles in a direct line with irregular shore, forming a coast of two hundred miles. These lakes, as may be judged from their formation, present unrivalled facilities for boating and camping. The principal varieties of the finny tribe are salmon trout, white-fish, bass and pickrel with maskinonge in adjacent lakes and streams. The chief point for " up the lakes," is at Gravenhurst. This town has just had a new outfit of fine brick hotels, the former five wooden hotels were swept away by the great conflagration of last September. The steamers depart twice daily during summer months, on the arrival of the trains of the Northern Division of the Grand Trunk Railway from all points; good meals are promptly served on board. The first resort of importance reached is Beaumaris, next Port Carling. Here, after passing through the lock, the Rosseau steamer heads for Windermere, Maplehurst and Rosseau, while the Port Cockburn steamer diverges to the left, calling at Ferndale, Port Sandfield, Redwood, Hamills, McLeans and Port Cockburn. A branch steamer usually makes the calls at Bracebridge, Oakland Park, Cleveland, Gregory and Craigilea during the busiest season. Additional local pleasure steamers will ply upon the lakes during the months of July and August, enabling hotel guests and others to take long or short outings, as they may desire. Also a tri-weekly boat to Bala Falls and intermediate places, on Mondays, Wednesdays and Fridays, affording a very pleasant sail of two hours each way. Daily stage coach connections to and from the Georgian Bay, via Port Cockburn and Parry Sound. The hotel men along this route are evincing a laudable ambition to keep abreast of the times. Several of the former houses have been enlarged since last season, and an additional new hotel erected at Windermere, also new hotel resorts have been established at Hamill's Bay and McLean's Bay on Lake Joseph, and at Bala, the outlet of Lake Muskoka.

## LOCAL BASE OF SUPPLIES.

CAMPERS and visitors of all classes can depend upon facilities for supplying themselves with almost any article in the way of provision supplies and general merchandise, at moderate prices, at Gravenhurst, Bracebridge, Port Carling, Windermere and Rosseau and to a smaller extent at other points on the Muskoka Lake route; at Parry Sound, Penetanguishene, Midland, Byng Inlet and French River, on the Georgian Bay route; and at Burk's Falls and Magnetawan village, on the upper Magnetawan route. See advertisements.

# RAILWAY ARRANGEMENTS.

## GRAND TRUNK RAILWAY (N. & N. W. Division.)

### Commencing on July 3rd (Special).

The Tri-weekly Fast Express Train with Parlor Cars up on Tuesdays, Thursdays and Saturdays, leaving Toronto at 10.20 a.m. ; down on Mondays, .Wednesdays and Fridays, leaving Gravenhurst at 5.50 p.m.

### REGULAR TRAIN SERVICE.

Leave Toronto....... 8.05 a.m., 11.45 a.m., 11.00 p.m. (Sleeping Car).
"     Hamilton ..... 7.05   "
"     Allandale.....11.20   "    3.10 p.m.   1.50 a.m.
"     Barrie'........11.23   "    3.30   "    1.52   "
"     Orillia........12.10 p.m.,   5.15   "    2.38   "
Arrive Gravenhurst,
    (Muskoka Wharf) 1.35   "     7.05   "    3.45   "
"     Penetanguishene 1.05   "    11.00   "
Depart Gravenhurst.   2.00   "    6.20 a.m., 11.50 p.m.
"     Penetanguishene 2.45   "    6.15   "

### Midland Division of Grand Trunk Railway.

Leave Toronto.......................... 7.35 a.m.. 4.35 p.m.
"     Port Hope...................... 7.00   "    3.45   "
"     Peterboro'..................... 8.20   "    5.10   "
"     Lindsay........................ 9.15   "    6.05   "
"     Orillia ........................11.58   "    8.58   "
Arrive Midland ...................... 1.30 p.m., 10.35   "
Depart    "     ...................... 6.20 a.m., 3.15   "

For Tickets and Rates apply to

P. J. SLATTER,              BARLOW CUMBERLAND,
   City Passenger Agent,           Ticket Agent,
     Cor. King & Yonge Sts., Toronto.    72 Yonge St., Toronto.

WM. EDGAR,              JOS. HICKSON,
   *Gen'l Passenger Agent.*           *General Manager.*

# MUSKOKA & NIPISSING NAVIGATION CO.—Muskoka Division.

The steamers "Nipissing" (new steel), "Kenozha," "Muskoka" and "Oriole," will ply as follows during the months of July and August, viz., twice daily to Beaumaris, Port Carling, Windermere, Maplehurst, Rosseau, Ferndale, Clevelands, Port Sandfield, Redwood, Yoho, Port Cockburn and intermediate places. Daily to Bracebridge. Tri-weekly on Tuesdays, Thursdays and Saturdays to Bala and intermediate places, in close connection with mail train. Tuesdays, Thursdays and Saturdays to Rosseau Falls, and on Tuesdays and Saturdays to Juddhaven from Rosseau. Mondays, Wednesdays and Fridays to Cloverport and Craigielea, in close connection with mail train. Close connections with all trains of the Grand Trunk Railway at Gravenhurst.

## GOING NORTH. — DAILY AND TWICE DAILY LINE.

| | A.M. | P.M. |
|---|---|---|
| Gravenhurst (Lake Muskoka) | 7.30 | 1.45 |
| Beachgrove do | *8.10 | 2.25 |
| Bracebridge (Muskoka River) | †9.00 | 3.45 |
| | | 3.15 |
| Beaumaris (Lake Muskoka) | 8.45 | 5.00 |
| Milford Bay do | *8.55 | *5.25 |
| Bala Outlet of do | ¶..... | ¶3.40 |
| Port Carling (between L. Rosseau and L. Muskoka) | 9.30 | 3.45 |
| | | 5.30 |
| Windermere (Lake Rosseau) | 11.00 | 5.45 |
| Penmans do | *11.15 | *6.00 |
| Maplehurst do | 11.45 | 6.30 |
| Rosseau do | 12.00 | 6.45 |
| Oakland Park do | *9.45 | *4.00 |
| Ferndale do | 10.00 | 4.15 |
| Cloverport do | | †4.40 |
| Clevelands do | 10.20 | 5.00 |
| Port Sandfield (between L. Joseph and L. Rosseau) | 10.15 | 4.30 |
| Redwood (Lake Joseph) | 10.35 | 4.45 |
| Craigielea do | | 5.15 |
| Yoho do | 11.30 | 5.30 |
| Stanley House do | 11.45 | 5.45 |
| Port Cockburn do | 12.00 | 6.30 |

## GOING SOUTH.

| | A.M. | P.M. |
|---|---|---|
| Port Cockburn (Lake Joseph) | 7.30 | 12.40 |
| Stanley House do | 7.45 | 1.00 |
| Yoho do | 8.00 | 1.10 |
| Craigielea do | ¶8.15 | 1.25 |
| Redwood do | 8.30 | 1.40 |
| Port Sandfield (between L. Joseph and L. Rosseau) | 9.00 | 2.05 |
| Clevelands (Lake Rosseau) | 9.00 | *2.30 |
| Cloverport do | ¶9.20 | |
| Ferndale do | 9.40 | 2.30 |
| Oakland Park do | *9.50 | |
| Rosseau do | 7.00 | 1.15 |
| Maplehurst do | 7.10 | 1.25 |
| Penmans do | *7.35 | |
| Windermere do | 8.00 | 2.00 |
| Port Carling (between L. Rosseau and L. Muskoka) | 8.30 | 2.45 |
| Bala Outlet and Lake Muskoka | 10.00 | |
| Milford Bay (Lake Muskoka) | ¶10.00 | 3.15 |
| Beaumaris do | 9.00 | 3.30 |
| Bracebridge (Muskoka River) | 10.30 | ¶4.30 |
| Beachgrove (Lake Muskoka) | 11.00 | |
| Gravenhurst do | 11.40 | |
| | 12.30 | 5.40 |

NOTE :—* Stop only on signal or by previous arrangement. ¶ Only on Tuesdays, Thursdays and Saturdays. † Mondays, Wednesdays and Fridays.

## TRI-WEEKLY LINE.

Leave Bala and intermediate places in close connection with Mail train on Tuesdays, Thursdays and Saturdays, Rosseau Falls from Rosseau at 7 a.m. on above days. Leave Cloverport and Craigielea on Mondays, Wednesdays and Fridays, in close connection with mail train.

## SEMI-WEEKLY LINE.

Juddhaven from Rosseau at 7 a.m. Tuesdays and Saturdays. Connections with Muskoka Special fast trains up on Tuesdays, Thursdays and Saturdays at 2.30 p.m., and down on Mondays, Wednesdays and Fridays at 5.50 p.m, Low Excursion Rates between all points.

## RAILWAY AND STAGE CONNECTIONS.

Gravenhurst and Bracebridge with the N. & N. W. Division of the Grand Trunk Railway Good Stage connections to Parry Sound on the Georgian Bay from Port Cockburn. Stage connections from Bracebridge to Baysville on Lake of Bays.

## GEORGIAN BAY DIVISION.

Daily per commodious and fast upper cabin steamer "F. B. Maxwell" (Capt. J. O'Donnell), from Penetanguishene and Midland on arrival of Mail trains to Parry Sound and intermediate places, Semiweekly on Mondays and Thursdays from Midland per staunch propeller "Imperial" (Capt. M. C. Cameron), to Byng Inlet and French River. Passengers for the above points will take the "Maxwell" at Penetanguishene or Midland to Parry Sound on Mondays, thence per "Imperial" on Thursdays. The "Imperial" will leave Midland at 5.00 a.m. for Byng Inlet and French River direct, passengers can go on board on Wednesday evening. For full particulars apply to McQuade, Penetanguishene or Midland, or to the undersigned.

## MAGNETAWAN DIVISION.

The combined paddle and screw steamer "Wenonah" (Capt. Wm. Kennedy), leaves Burk's Falls (Railway Station of the N. & N. W. Ry. Div. of G.T.R.) daily at 7 a.m. for Magnetawan Village, Ahmic Harbor and intermediate places, returning at 5 p.m. For particulars apply to R. H. Menzies and Capt. Kennedy, at Burk's Falls, or to the undersigned.

## A. P. COCKBURN,

*General Manager,*

*GRAVENHURST.*

## J. A. LINK,

*Sec'y-Treas.,*

*GRAVENHURST.*

# Tariff of Tourist Fares from 15th June to 30th Sept., valid to return up to 30th October, and subject to cancellation at option of Grand Trunk Railway Company.

| TO AND RETURN. | From Montreal. | From Toronto, Davenport, Georgetown, Milton, Burlington and Hamilton. | |
|---|---|---|---|
| All Round Muskoka Lakes... .... ........ | $18 60 | $7 00 | Muskoka Division. |
| Bracebridge (all rail or boat and rail)........ | 16 85 | 5 00 | |
| Beaumaris...... ................ ........ | .. .. | 5 40 | |
| Port Carling, Bala and Torrence............ | 17 10 | £ 50 | |
| Windermere, Port Sandfield, Clevelands, Gregory, Ferndale House and Cloverport | 17 35 | 5 75 | |
| Rosseau................................ .. | 17 85 | 6 00 | |
| Port Cockburn, Lake Joseph ............. ... | 18 10 | 6 50 | |
| Parry Sound (via Penetang or Midland)...... | .. .. | 7 50 | Georgian Bay Division |
| "  (via Muskoka, return via Penetang or Midland or vice versa | .. .. | 8 00 | |
| Byng Inlet (meals and state-rooms included).. | .. .. | 10 00 | |
| French River  "  "  "  .. | .. .. | 12 00 | |
| Magnetawan........... ...  Steamer from Burk's Falls. | .. .. | 8 35 | Magnetawan Division |
| Port Anson (Depot Farm).. | .. .. | 8 60 | |
| Ahmic Harbor ........... | .. .. | 9 10 | |

# TICKET AGENCIES.

TORONTO.--P. J. SLATTER, City Agent G.T.R., Cor. King and Yonge
B. CUMBERLAND, Ticket Agent, N. & N. Div., 72 Yonge St.
Streets, and the G.T.R. Stations in the City.

HAMILTON.—W. J. GRANT, No. 8 James St. South and No. 33 Main
Street Office.
CHAS. MORGAN, No. 11 James St. North, and the Railway Stations.

CHICAGO, ILL.—LAKE SUPERIOR & LAKE MICHIGAN TRANSIT CO.

ROCHESTER, N.Y.—LEWIS & CO,

BUFFALO.—T. D. SHERADIAN, Washington Street.

Tickets can also be procured at the Agencies of the Grand Trunk Railway,
and at the principal Towns and Cities of Canada and the
United States.

# VACATION IN MUSKOKA.

BY REV. JOHN POTTS, D.D., PRESIDENT OF TORONTO
CONFERENCE.

WHERE will you spend your holidays? is a question often asked as we enter into the leafy month of June. How many are the answers to such a question.

One says Long Branch, one Newport, one Orchard Beach—another says Murray Bay, or Cacouna, or Little Metis. To the above question, an increasing number will promptly respond, Muskoka. And why not?

Within easy distance of Toronto and Hamilton, there is a region of great beauty, which ought to be better known by all who are interested in the scenery of their country, and by all who are on the look out for a convenient place to spend an inexpensive holiday.

Leaving Toronto at 8 a.m. by the Northern Division of the Grand Trunk, you reach Muskoka wharf, at Gravenhurst, a little after two o'clock.

Two steamers will be found lying at the wharf, one bound for Lake Joseph and the other for Rosseau.

Both run through Lake Muskoka to Port Carling.

One of them runs up through the charming Lake Joseph to Port Cockburn. This lake is dotted with islands, many of them owned and inhabited by citizens of Toronto.

The other steamer runs through Lake Rosseau, calling at Windermere, and reaching Rosseau often by eight o'clock.

2

I think the first place of beauty must be assigned to Joseph, while Rosseau is only second to Joseph in variety and beauty of scenery.

LAKE JOSEPH.

All through these charming waters may be found modest hotels at reasonable rates, and good boarding-houses, which do not overtax those of moderate income. The table is well provided, not with all the delicacies of the season, but with good substantial fare. One of the attractions of Muskoka is, that you are not in bondage to the wiles of fashion which govern the more pretentious summer resorts of the American side, and one or two in our own Dominion.

It seems to be a paradise for children, judging from their enjoyment, and parents rejoice to see their bairns improving in colour and appetite. The recreation of boating is one of the features of Windermere, and while fishing affords pleasure to the gentlemen, it supplies the table with delicious bass and pickerel.

More and more, these Muskoka regions will attract the toilers of our Ontario towns and cities, until every island shall be inhabited, and the busy brain and muscle workers shall be nerved both in mind and body, and better fitted to resume the earnest work of life. One thing that impresses the Muskoka tourist, is that Canadians need not leave their own country for varied and beautiful scenery. For a long time we pointed with pride to the Thousand Islands of the magnificent St. Lawrence; and in our limited knowledge of Canadian scenery supposed that the well-known tourist route was unequalled in all the Dominion. We do no injustice to the St. Lawrence, when we say it must take a second place to Muskoka in the same class of scenery.

The cottages generally are simple in architecture, not costing more than from $300 to $500, while many cost less than the former sum, and a few much more.

Perhaps the finest residence on these lakes is that of W. E. Sanford, Esq., of Hamilton, which is on an island in Rosseau not far from Port Carling. There are some lovely points near Windermere, which in many respects are preferable to islands, especially to those not expert at boating.

In this busy age, all workers should arrange to take a few weeks' outing, and I know of no place to be preferred to one or other of these Muskoka lakes.

---

## A HOLIDAY IN PARRY SOUND.

### SIGHTS AND SCENES IN THE SWITZERLAND OF CANADA.

LEAVING Hamilton with the 7 a.m. train for Penetang, we embarked at noon on board the fine steamer Maxwell, Capt. O'Donnell; sailed around the Reformatory Point into Midland, then north through the great Georgian Bay among the 3,000 islands to Parry Harbor, in time for supper. Ina, one of our party, who has seen the St. Lawrence thousand islands in their best summer garb, sailed through Lakes Huron and Superior, and was delighted with the grand, bold, rugged rocks and cliffs, acknowledged this five hours' trip the finest scenery of its kind she ever beheld. Parry Harbor and the Sound, two villages, have their large hotels, filled to overflowing with summer tourists—the *elite* of New England and Canadian cities. A carriage ride out about six miles toward

Lake Joseph on the Parry Sound road, then one mile to the right, brought us to the ranch where we lived with Mr. and Mrs. Jas. S. Miller, managers of the ranch. It was dark. Next morning shortly after sunrise we took in our situation and surroundings. The house is small, but cosy and pleasant, the front nearly covered with climbing vines and roses. In front a pretty flower garden, at the rear an excellent vegetable garden ; surrounded on three sides by a fine field of nearly ripened oats. It is on the side of a hill, gently sloping two ways to Otter lake and over-looking more than a mile each way, north and south of the lake. Just below at the foot of the hill a corduroy bridge crosses the narrows from west to east. The grass was wet with a heavy dew, which sparkled and glistened in the morning sun. The whole looked like a fairy place. Here we were daily regaled with rich, fresh milk, home-made bread and butter, prize maple syrup, choice lamb, fresh fish of our own catch, wild strawberry and raspberry preserves, and ripe, luscious, native plums, and could gather blue and thimble berries in thousands. We often ate five times a day and the children asked for snacks between. We had two ordinary, substantial row-boats, each sufficient for a whole family, when we trolled for pike, bass and salmon. Neither of our party ever caught fish by troll, and this new sport to us was glorious. Little Lillie, not five years old, caught several and unassisted hauled in " her own self " a two-pound bass, her ma holding her to guard against accident. Mary, ten years old, was the luckiest in catching large- fish ; Mr. Miller, who had charge of that boat, hauled them for her. We reserved for own use the average size bass only, the large bass and all pike were given to the pigs. We caught no salmon; we were told they kept in the deepest and coolest parts of the lake in the hot weather. The two boats kept within speaking distance of each other, and the cheers and enthusiastic yelling that continually occurred when a fish was caught would do justice to as many Comanche Indians. The lake is somewhat the shape of a horseshoe, 400 yards to 1½ miles wide, 50 to 150 feet deep. Opposite side from the ranch is deeply indented with enchanting narrow-winding bays, bordered by high rough and rugged granite rocks, almost hidden by the green trees growing up their sides. The many islands from one-half to four or five acres each dot the lake, all green and pretty ; the campers' fire has not devastated any of them as in the Georgian Bay or the Muskoka Lakes. From the foot of the lake to the landing on Parry Sound road is a pretty straight away sail of about eight and a-half miles, in through and among lovely islands, grand and interesting; a scenery that equals the renowned lakes of Killarney or the famous lochs of Scotland, made famous by song and thrilling story. This lake is the big link in the chain of the proposed canoe route for next summer tourists. Here we might picture for the pleasure seekers' participation the gallant little steamer "Otter" with its twenty tourists, gliding noiselessly through the clear, deep waters in and around green islands on the loveliest lake in the district. The hills come sweeping gracefully down in wooded bluffs, or bold projecting rocks and

23

MAKING A PORTAGE.

rolling meadows, till the deep, blue waters of the cool lake lap the shore and murmur on the beach a low, crooning monotone of poetic dreaminess. At the foot of the lake quite close to the canoe portage, mother earth in the depth of ages past with a mighty upheaval, left a granite mountain, serried and grand, a monument of her mighty throes. Here the shady birch and maple, the green pine and balsam, have thrust their roots into the deep crevices of the everlasting rocks. The sight is magnificent! The placid, calm mirror, water coloured silk, ever changing, and the perfect reflection of the tall, green mountain in the water, adds to its grandeur. To the left, up and over the great farm, the glowing tints of a Parry Sound summer nestle in the dusky dells with its gurgling springs and lakelets, suggest that the heavens have dropped to earth and met in loving embrace the surrounding scenery. A deep sense of the beauty of the scene falls on all, and for a time one is subdued as he drinks deep of the spirit of loveliness which broods on all around. The scene is grand beyond all conception and silenced all expressions of admiration. In the mountain's august presence we unconsciously uncover the head and exclaim, "Great! Grand! Glorious! Eternal!" We turn homeward, and the ruffling breath of an evening zephyr stirs up the pulses of the pretty lake. The shadows and reflections flit and shimmer from shore to shore, and island to island. I cannot do the subject justice; you must be there personally and experience as we have the healthy, gratifying, exhilirating pleasures of two weeks' holidays at the ranch in Parry Sound.                    DE. JAY.

# ALDERMANIC TRIP TO BURK'S FALLS.

BURK'S FALLS is situated on the Magnetawan, a stream which reaches Georgian Bay at Byng Inlet. A number of lakes lie along its course, the principal which are Cecebe and Ahmic lakes. The river from Burk's Falls to Cecebe lake is naturally navigable ; and a lock at the village of Magnetawan secures communication with Ahmic lake, so that the total length of navigable waters is fully forty miles. The Muskoka and Nipissing Navigation company has placed on this route a very comfortable boat, the Wenonah, commanded by Captain Kennedy ; and on Tuesday morning Mayor McKay led his party on board this vessel for a trip which lasted all day. It is really one of the most delightful excursions which can possibly be made in the whole of the picturesque Muskoka country. For several miles below Burk's Falls the river averages more than 100 feet in width. It winds in and out through the almost unbroken forest, its banks lined to the water's edge with maple, birch and other hardwood trees, thickly interspersed with the tall, graceful cones of spruce, balsam and hemlock, and the graceful, feathery fronds of the tamarack The water lies still and unruffled in the solemn quiet of the primitive woods ; and the shadows of the trees are as dictinctly reflected in the calm mirror of the water as though the forest were double. So narrow is the stream that at certain points one may pick leaves from the trees as the boat steams down the river.

Ceccbe lake is filled with islands—a double of the Muskoka lakes on a somewhat smaller scale. At Magnetawan a' lock has just been finished, which permits the boat to descend into Lake Ahmic, another charming sheet of water. Ahmic harbor, at the foot of the lake, is the end of the journey, and thence the boat returned to Burk's Falls. Captain Kennedy is a most courteous and obliging man, and showed every possible attention to his guests. The charge for the round trip, including a comfortable and substantial dinner on the boat, is two dollars; and certainly the excursion is one of the cheapest to be had. The *Wenonah* can carry comfortably at least a hundred passengers.

On Thursday morning the party returned to Gravenhurst, and thence took passage for Rosseau by the *Kenozha*, Captain Henry; and next morning returned to Port Carling, at the southern extremity of Lake Rosseau. The majority of the excursionists at once took boat for Port Cockburn, at the head of Lake Joseph, returning to Port Carling in the evening, having had a delightful trip through Lake Joseph. Others remained at Port Carling, some of whom went fishing, with indifferent success. Among the visitors to Port Carling is Mrs. Judge O'Reilly, who thinks it the most pleasant resort on the lakes.

On Friday morning the party took the *Kenozha* for home. The boat went up the river to Bracebridge on the way to Gravenhurst, and thus the majority of the party had an opportunity to see Lakes Cecebe, Ahmic,

uskoka, Rosseau, and Joseph, besides considerable
retches of the Muskoka and Magnetawan rivers.

The excursionists were also unanimous in their
)inion that the presence of ladies added greatly to
ie enjoyment of the whole party and in expressing
hope that future excursions of the sort would be
onoured and graced by ladies.

ON THE RIVER BELOW PORT CARLING.

It is very true that a visit to Muskoka should not
)e made in so hasty and hurried a manner. If one
lesires rest and enjoyment he should be able wholly
:o throw off the idea that time has any claim upon
iim or any control over his movements. His busi-
iess is not to hasten with eager and restless steps

from one scene of beauty to another, but to linger and dream away the idle hours in one place till he becomes saturated with the beauty of his surroundings and forgets that business and worry and unloveliness have any place in the wide creation of God. Several days are required by the ordinary man to shake off the feeling that he must hurry down to the office or the shop. But that feeling must be shaken off before he is in condition to enjoy the Muskoka scenery. Then he can begin to realize that he is in another world—a world fresh and unspotted from the hands of its great Architect ; and as he takes in fresh life with every inspiration of the pure air of the country his spiritual nature takes in new life from very near to the fountain. Perhaps the man may catch no fish, but he catches the beauty of nature, the whisper that falls across Muskoka's inlets and woods, dropping from the presence of the Eternal, and his eye takes in gleams of light reflected by her waters from the gleaming gates of heaven. The pulses of the night amid the solemn grandeur of the forests fill him with mysterious awe and a reverence unknown to cities teaches him humbleness and reverence as he stands in the mysterious temples built by the finger of God. But, as has been said, one must wait till the dust of the city be blown from him before he can enter fully into the mysteries which lie around him, feel his heart lift in gratitude to the beneficent Maker of it all and feel himself enlightened and lifted up by communion with nature. The Hamilton party had glimpses of the good that is in Muskoka, but could not tarry to enjoy it.—*Hamilton Spectator*.

FROM THE " WEEK " AUG. 25, 1887.

SOME hundred miles or so north of Toronto, at a few hours' distance by boat and rail, is a tract of country as large as Belgium, which, from its elevation above the general level, is aptly called the Highlands of Ontario. Like the Scottish Highlands, the land is one of lake and woodland : numerous sheets of water, varying in size from the lakelet to the miniature sea, dot the well-timbered expanse ; but from out the number a group of three only stand prominent for considerable size, being also not very dissimilar from one another in extent. These are Lakes Muskoka, Joseph, and Rosseau, which crown the Highlands, covering an extent of some forty miles in length by ten in width.

No majestic mountain keeps watch over the dark waters of these lakes ; from no cloud-wrapt giant can we survey the scene of marvellous beauty that lies here. The bosom of these lakes is studded with islet-gems strewn thick on the limpid waters. But to see them we must traverse the watery paths that are spread before the traveller's feet from Gravenhurst to Port Cockburn on the one hand and Rosseau on the other.

Leaving Gravenhurst, and passing on to the further end of Lake Rosseau, where, opposite the village of that name, at the distance of about a mile, is a bold promontory jutting out into the lake, from which may be had such a view of the neighbourhood as may serve to convey as good an idea of the character of the Muskoka region as can be obtained anywhere.

From Maplehurst we overlook many a wood-crowned islet and cape, whose rugged sides and huge rocky gables frowning at the waters laving their base bear in the finger-prints of the floods, the marks of hoary age. Near by are " islets on islets still," while the far distance is crowned with ranges of pine-clad hills. As becomes the domain of a young democracy, no one hill there rears its proud top over others—all are on the same plane.

No " haughty peerage of attendant mountains " guard these lakes, thrusting their proud fronts into the rain-charged clouds ; yet hills there are of considerable elevation, whose valleys, however, are hid from sight. The traveller indeed passes by a watery path from hill-top to hill-top ; while beneath the waters at his feet, hundred of fathoms down, at the level of Lake Ontario, are spread valleys whose too copious springs have drowned what else were meadows. Very rich must these submerged bottoms be. The rains of ages have left the rocky summits of many of the hills bare, washing the rich soil into the hidden valleys ; yet wherever the wooded heights have held sufficient soil a remarkable and almost tropical luxuriance of vegetable growth is seen. Turning for a moment from the lake we see patches, small it is true, of excellent arable land, embedded in forests of maple, birch, bass, elm, and oak, whose lofty tops attest a remarkable degree of fertility in the soil ; while the richest and most tempting pasturage is spread before grazing cattle. A marked feature, however, of Muskoka is the prevalence of enormous rocks or boulders scattered over the land, which meet the eye in most unexpected laces, and detract much from its agricultural value. Yet the abundance and purity of the water throughout this whole district, the clear sky, and bright sunshine, tempered by the brisk-moving waters of the lakes, may make it for beast as well as man the envy of many much lauded districts to the south of Canada.

Skirting the shore along Maplehurst, in one of the gondolas that are almost a necessity to life in this Canadian Venice, we strike across a shallow bay, past a small cape, into another and larger bay, whose entrance is guarded by two islands, now but dimly seen through the mist. The shore beside us is here and there strewn with rocks, torn into fragments by uprooted trees, to which they have once afforded in their crevices a scant though secure hold ; here is one of these ungrateful children of the forest, overturned in some storm, holding aloft in its roots a mass of rock, as if in triumphant mockery. No storms greatly disturb the placid waters of these lakes ; yet in the course of ages the margin has been strewn with the *debris* of many an elemental war.

The character of the whole region is peaceful and restful, rather than imposing or magnificent. In this bay, however, on this misty afternoon, a grand sight greets us. The scene has a Turneresque effect, resembling a well-known picture of an early foggy morning. The land, the water, the sky, are harmoniously blended in varying shades of gray, presenting a most weird appearance ; while a boat, creeping along in the shadow of the hither shore of an island—a shadow scarcely distinguishable from the substance—stands out as if suspended in mid-air.

On a still day a similar effect is seen to perfection on a small river that falls into the lake, on the opposite side from Maplehurst, winding inland for some miles like a silver thread between its green banks. White

ON THE SHADOW RIVER.

Oak Creek, or Shadow River as it is locally named, is in itself alone well worth a visit from afar. To those on the spot, its surpassing loveliness in places, new scenes of surprising beauty breaking on the view at almost every turn of the river, is a lasting attraction. A peculiarity that distinguishes it besides is indi-

cated by its second name. As in the late afternoon we
glide along its silver surface, marking for a moment
the heavy flight of a crane overhead, which our
approach has disturbed, we are dazzled by an illusion
caused by the reflection of the trees and luxurious
undergrowth beside the stream, which show in the
still water like a hanging garden, the moss and fern-
covered verge duplicated and reversed, the trees striking their tall tops into a nether sky, so that it is next
to impossible to distinguish the water line, and puzz-
ling to find the channel out of this Elysium. Nature
indeed appears so lovely here that in very pride she
reflects her own beauty in this mirror.

Beside the entrance to Shadow River, on the right
is a pine grove, whose scented air and cool shades are
a delicious refreshment on warm afternoons. In the
woods, too, about Maplehurst are several delightful
walks through green lanes, where numerous partridges,
started from their covert by our tread, whirr in all
directions about us ; while deer afford excellent sport
later in the year. The numerous woods and lakes in
the neighbourhood, being out of the beaten track, are
practically unhunted and unfished. It is thought that
the game has been driven into this district, where are
no railways nearer than twenty-two miles, by the
opening of the C. P. R. to the north.

The sound of the " lapping wavelets" grown familiar
during a fortnight's stay here, will continue to echo
pleasantly in memory when the writer is far from
Muskoka ; the scenery he has here attempted to trace
in outline will, though distant in time and space, abide
crystallised as a delightful mental picture. And in

3

closing this paper he would commend these fair and noble lakes to the attention of all able to appreciate the glory and beauty of nature, confident that in few other places in Canada will both be found in so great abundance.

J. H. MENZIES.

---

# THRILLING EXPEDITION UP NORTH.

WHEN, in your wisdom, Mr. Grip, you supplied me with a complete camping and fishing outfit, and despatched me to the distant region of Parry Sound, to investigate and report upon that section of the country, I did not quail at the undertaking. You observed no tremor in my manly form, nor pallor on my firm-set lips. It would ill-become a Journalist of my standing and experience, to blanch at such a trial in this day of terrific though chestnutty exploits in central prison cells. At the word of command I boldly set off on my expedition, and up to the present time I am proud to say I have, by dogged perseverance and unshrinking courage, overcome every danger and difficulty that has beset my path. The first stage of my journey (as you will see by consulting the Government map in the Crown Lands Department,) was by rail to Penetanguishene. The truly brave are always modest, and I do not care to expatiate upon the steadiness of nerve with which I sat in the car and gazed calmly at the passing landscape. But I think I may safely say, that nobody who saw me, would for a moment suppose that I held my life in my hands. It is only fair to admit that the spirit of hardihood exhibited by your representative, was shared to some extent by all his travelling companions. The conductor of the train was not merely composed, he was positively jolly, and so reckless was he of danger that I saw him, on several occasions, actually walk from one car to another. Upon making enquiry as to the biography of this brave man (whose name was Pim,) I was informed that he was really no braver than other Northern railway men, and that they are oblivious of danger for the reason that the road is considered uncommonly safe. After hearing this my nerves became even steadier than before. In due time— after what I may call a pleasant trip, notwithstanding that it was the first stage of a perilous expedition—we arrived at the Penetanguishene wharf, where we found the steamer *Maxwell* waiting to receive us. The boat is one of the Muskoka Navigation Company's fleet, and like the head manager of the organization, Mr. A. P. Cockburn, they are staunch, solid, and full of " go." Having learned this from a reliable authority, I went on board without hesitation, although the gang-plank was only two feet wide. I found the vessel in all respects well equipped for the thrilling expedition upon which I was embarked. The dining saloon was large and nicely furnished with easy chairs and sofas, and the adjoining parlor contained a very good piano. The purser had an exceedingly civilized look, and I found it hard to believe that I was so far from Toronto—the intellectual centre. A glance at my ticket assured me, however, that I was veritably on my way to the wild, free, rock-bound coast of the Georgian Bay, where so many brave men have perished in horrible tortures at the hands of the savage red-men. Before the steamer left the wharf, one of the natives pointed out to me the spot where Brébœuf and Lallemant were massacred, but I never quailed for an instant. When you are in for it, what is the use of quailing? The baggage having been taken on board the stern line was cast off, at the suggestion of our captain, and away she went. After a run of four or five miles, we touched at Midland, and having transacted our business there, we set sail once more—this time for Parry Sound direct. Somehow, my nerves had now become perfectly callous. I was an entire stranger to fear—didn't remember ever to have met him. Here I was, going with every turn of the paddle-wheels nearer and nearer to my destination, and yet utterly oblivious of all danger. In fact I could and really did enjoy the scenery—and such scenery! A man on his way to the very scaffold would enjoy it. Islands by the thousand each trying to look prettier than its neighbour. Mr. Grip, you really must send your poet up here to do this scenery justice; I would only profane the subject with my clumsy hand. But wouldn't I like to see old Alex. McLachlan gazing at it, and afterwards read what he thought of it? It might be dangerous though. Two to one, the Grand

Old Man would jump overboard in his ecstasy. Well, thus we wended our way all afternoon and up to ten o'clock in the evening through a maze of beauty, stopping every now and then to put off provisions into small boats that shot out to meet us along the route, for these islands are well populated in the summer season by a race of dusky, but intelligent and happy beings, in flannel shirts and knickerbockers, who are known as "campers." At the hour named we entered the harbour of Parry Sound, and in due time found ourselves on *terra firma*, and still our hearts never quailed!

I say that when I found myself actually upon the scene of action, I still retained all my wonted bravery. Nothing could be done in the way of thrilling adventure until morning, however, and under all the circumstances I thought it advisable that I should spend the interim in bed. I couldn't just then hit upon any better plan of spending it, though I confess the idea of a " bed " was somewhat humiliating to me. Had I not come to this faraway district upon an *expedition ?* " Bed " had a summer-resort sound ; I would have thought it more in accordance with the fitness of things had I been able to contemplate a few evergreen boughs thrown together behind a sheltering rock as a couch for the night, but it was too dark for me to find the boughs. I accordingly allowed myself—not without inward protest—to be led by a friendly guide along the waggon path to the " Belvidere." This, I may explain, is the name of a big hotel, standing upon a remarkably high, rocky bluff, overlooking the Sound. I can hardly describe to you the chagrin with which I learned of the existence of this hotel, and of the further fact that at the very moment of my arrival it was well filled with guests, from Toronto, New York, Boston, etc. The chances of thrilling adventures in the vicinity of a big hotel seemed to me pretty slim. I began to feel that I had been basely trifled with, and the comfortable idea that I was a second Stanley threatened to desert me. The only thing I could do by way of a protest against the hotel was to refuse to sleep at it. "I came here on an expedition, not on a summer holiday," I said to my guide with some asperity, "that

I want to rough it. Isn't there some uncomfortable place where I can pass the night—some place where my fitful slumbers can be broken by the growl of bears and the howl of hungry wolves?"

"Oh, if that's what you want, just follow me," he replied, and I could see by the gleam of the lantern in his hand that his frame trembled. We left the vicinity of the hotel and plunged into the darkness, going down several flights of steps in the inside of the rock. On,

on we went, I know not how far, through sand, ankle
deep. At last we stopped at what appeared to be a
hut. Opening the door, the guide led me inside and
pointed out a pallet of Indian straw in one corner.
" Ah," said I, gleefully, " that's more like the thing !
Good-night, my man." He left, and I immediately
retired to rest. For a time my busy brain was engaged
in depicting my surroundings, which as yet I had not
seen, but I was too tired to do any clear thinking.
Amid a confusion of ideas, involving tangled under-
brush, dense forests, frowning rocks, gloomy caverns,
hissing reptiles and ferocious wild beasts, I dropped
off to sleep. How long I slept I know not, but I suddenly found myself sitting bolt upright and listening
to a series of noises which had effectually dispelled my
slumber. A harsh, barking noise, followed by an
alarmed bleating sound and the muddled footfall of
two denizens of the forest, clearly to my now alert
faculties a deer pursued by a wolf ! They were now
close to my hut, and dashed right past the door as I
arose. Seizing my gun I peered through the window,
but I saw nothing for pitchy darkness without. In
the distance I still heard the trampling of the fright-
ened deer and the growl of its ruthless pursuer. I
retired once more, but with pleasurable anticipations
of the sport which awaited me in the morning in this
wild land. When I awoke it was broad day, and just
as the sun dispels the mists of the valley, so it chased
away all my cherished hopes. What did I find ?
That I was not in a hut at all, but in an elegant little
two-storey cottage, within a romantic enclosure known
as the Parry Sound Camp Ground, a few hundred

yards below the "Belvidere," bordered on three sides by a pretty grove, and sloping gently to the boat-houses and bathing beach in the fourth direction. My deer and wolf of the night vision materialized in themselves in the shape of a calf and a little dog, belonging to one of the neighbours. Close to my cottage there were three others of the same pattern, all occupied by persons fully as civilized as myself, while in other parts of the ground were more humble camping buildings surrounding the platforms and benches of the auditorium. I was the most disappointed and exasperated adventurer, Mr. Grip, that ever went abroad to represent your enterprising journal in a wild district. My dream of thrilling exploit was pretty well over, and it vanished altogether when I had more fully taken in my surroundings. I found, for instance, that the thriving town of Parry Sound was within ten minutes walk through the grove, and that the butcher, baker, ice-dealer and talie-man were in the habit of making daily calls at the cottages. There was no question about it, I was in the very heart of civilization and refinement, and I say here as I said to Mr. Erastus Jackson (who with his family I found residing in a cottage close by), Parry Sound, as a place for terrific adventures with Indians and wild beasts, is not what it was two centuries ago! I am not the man, however, to give way to futile regrets, Mr. Grip, as you know. I accepted the situation with my customary philosophy, I could not have thrilling adventure, but I found there was any amount of fun, health and appetite to be had, and I thought it my duty, under the circumstances, to get what I could of these good things. So, up to the present writing, I have sought to banish my feeling of disappointment in a round of fishing, yachting (both sail and steam), boating, bathing, shooting, blue-berry-ing, camp-visiting, etc., etc., and I have succeeded pretty well. For a man who likes these things as summer recreations, and who isn't troubled with an overmastering desire to hunt bears and hyenas, I really think Parry Sound as a district may be called a success. To be perfectly candid, I do not know of any place fit to compare with it, and I find it very hard to make up my mind to go home. I am going, however, Mr. Grip, the week after next.—*From "Grip."*

## MAGNETAWAN RIVER AND AHMIC LAKE.

The glory of Muskoka lies as much in its rivers as in its lakes—in the wild and untamed Muskoka river, with its picturesque waterfalls, in the placidity of the Shadow River, typical of all that is peaceful and rest-ful, in the beauties of the Moose River falling over a succession of rocky clifts until it reaches Georgian Bay. No less beautiful than its companions to the south is the Magnetawan River, which stretches for miles from the thriving village of Burk's Falls to Ahmic Lake on the west. Burk's Falls is on the line of railway running to North Bay, and the omnibus in waiting will take the passengers to one of the three new hotels. Tied to the wharf is the steamer of the Muskoka Navigation Company which makes an early start for its day's journey. As soon as the village with its neatly painted frame houses covering the hillside is lost to view, the river springs a succession of surprises upon the tourist. With a course so erratic that the sharpest curves are made, any possibility of monotony is removed, and the eye is kept on the alert for new vistas and ever changing ˙ aspects. The steamer is provided with a propeller blade as well as side-wheels, both being required in navigating the tortuous stream, whose banks are covered with a dense

CAMPING ON AHMIC LAKE.

growth of trees, and whose waters are of a colour marvellously rich and dark. Wild game abounds and the deck hands while away their spare time in taking aim at passing flocks of wild-duck. The river, too, is a practically unexplored Eldorado for the lover of fishing, its depths hiding swarms of finny beauties.

The village of Magnetawan is next reached, where a Government lock admits the vessel to Ahmic

Lake, a lovely sheet of water dotted with picturesquely shaped islands which reflect their wood-covered outlines in the waters below; indeed, this lake is equal in beauty to any Muskoka can boast of, and the visitor is entranced, until the little hamlet of Ahmic Harbor, the end of our journey westward, is reached.   On the return trip, in the cool of the afternoon, one sees the lake and river in still more attractive beauty.   The glittering sunshine of the forenoon which had flooded the river's surface, revealing every nook and corner, is now retreating toward the western horizon, leaving watery solitudes and mysterious caves and retreats where life seems to be suspended.   A spell seems to come over the onlooker which is only broken as the steamer emerges again in view of our starting point, where a tempting meal awaits us.

FRANK YEIGH.

FROM THE DUMFRIES REFORMER.

MANY Canadians have to revise their estimate of their country's resources in many particulars, but in none probably more than its numerous beautiful summer resorts.   The beauty of the St. Lawrence and the Thousand Islands, the grandeur of the Saguenay, and the rugged scenery of the shores of Lake Superior, have excited the admiration of many foreign travellers; but probably none of these combine so many attractive features to the tourist, the sportsman, and the health seeker, as the Muskoka Lakes region, which is within a few hours' journey of Toronto or Galt.

There has been an unusually large influx of tourists into that district this summer, and it is impossible to find a more lovely and enjoyable sail than the round trip by the Muskoka and Nipissing Company's steamers over Lakes Muskoka, Rosseau and Joseph. Mr. A. P. Cockburn, who is manager of the line, is one of the most popular and obliging of men and their fleet of boats, although not very large, is exceedingly handsome and well equipped. The lakes are dotted all over with islands, of all sizes and shapes, making up a picture of natural beauty which might put the Grecian Archipelago to the blush. Most of the islands are covered profusely with our principal Canadian trees and other vegetation down to the water's edge, and their brilliant foliage can often be seen trailing in the sparkling waters.

A large number of the islands are now inhabited, and beautiful summer villas crown the most prominent points. These are mainly owned by Torontonians, but Montreal, Hamilton, Galt, Woodstock and many other places are represented. The water around the islands is generally deep, each one inhabited has its rustic wharf, and flags are to be seen flying from every house and tent. The latter are quite numerous, and are largely adopted by the numerous large clubs of Americans who resort to Muskoka every summer. They evidently have a jolly time in these camps, some coming prepared with good çooks and all the luxuries necessary to make an enjoyable summer outing.

The best way to reach this delightful region, is to go by rail to Gravenhurst, then take the Muskoka and Nipissing Co.'s boats to the head of Lake Muskoka

ON LAKE MUSKOKA.

to Port Carling. There are locks here which enable
the boats to reach Lake Rosseau, and a very good
plan is to go at once to the head of this lake. There
are good hotels there, and also at Beaumaris, Windermere, and other points on the way up. The Shadow
river here, is a sight which should not be omitted.
Returning to Port Carling again, the new steamer
Nipissing can be taken for the trip up Lake Joseph,
which is entered from Rosseau by a cut called Port
Sandfield, connecting these two charming sheets of
water. Here there is a splendid hotel (Prospect
House), which can accommodate three hundred guests.
At the head of Lake Joseph is another large hotel
called the Summit House, which occupies one of the
most pleasing sites on the main land. It is a disputed
point which of these two lakes is the more beautiful
Both have their warm partizans, both have special
attractions, but most visitors find it about as difficult
to decide between them as the beau with the two
sweethearts, who exclaimed :—

"How happy he could be with either,
Were 'tother dear charmer away."

That the Muskoka Lakes must take front rank
among Canadian summer resorts, can hardly be
doubted by anyone who has been there. The region
is close at hand, its waters are not disturbed by dangerous storms like Huron or Superior, and the scenery
is at once picturesque and pleasing. Add to this that
it is a perfect paradise for the fisherman, the gunner
and the canoeist, and enough has been said to show
that it is one of the most attractive spots on the continent to which the tourist, whether seeking after
health or adventure, can turn his wayward footsteps.

# BY AN OLD CAMPER.

WHEN the thermometer stands at 80° in the shade, and those whom fortune has favoured with time and means at their disposal, are discussing the question where to go to enjoy a rest from the cares of business and a pleasant relief from the dust and heat of the crowded city, I would advise them instead of going to the populous watering-places to plunge into a vortex of fashionable dissipation, where rest in its true sense is only a delusion, to try the cool refreshing breezes of the Georgian Bay, where they can pass a few weeks pleasantly at a very small cost. They can take possession of an island and, like Robinson Crusoe, be "monarch of all they survey." If fond of piscatorial pursuits, they can here enjoy themselves to the fullest extent, and with rod and line pull the finny tribe from their watery homes ; black bass, weighing from two to four pounds, that would have delighted old Izaak Walton himself; or, if this seems too laborious, they can procure a boat and a man to row, and reclining luxuriously in the stern, skim round the islands or through deep and intricate channels, trolling for pike, muskallonge, or salmon trout. If lovers of nature in its wild picturesque ruggedness, they will find here an ample field for enjoyment, as island after island presents itself to view, covered with pine or cedar, rendered more picturesque by the sheen of white poplar glinting through their sombre shadows ; again, a bay of inimitable beauty bursts on their vision, whose shores are covered with a thick growth of trees, the green foliage of which, bowing down, appears to kiss the dark water beneath, the whole presenting a view to delight the eye òf the artist. Again, passing an island which raises its head like "the old man of the sea," grey with different varieties of moss which clothe its summit, they glide into a channel, whose walls of rock threaten every moment to meet and bar their further progress; but as they glide on, open their portals and allow the boat to pursue its tortuous way through a labyrinth, almost as intricate as that which Henry II. had to follow to reach the bower of his fair Rosamond

A few weeks spent among these islands soon remove all feeling of lassitude, and like Antæus when he touched his mother earth, those who visit them will return invigorated and ready to resume the tasks and cares of life.

The "Million Isles," stretching from the County of Simcoe to Sault Ste. Marie, are only a few hours' ride from the principal cities of Ontario, almost at their doors. The tourist can go by rail to the old town of Penetanguishene, the appropriate Huron name for "rolling sand," or to the village of Midland, rapidly growing into importance. Here he will find himself on historic ground, for it was once the seat of the mighty Huron nation, whose villages were scattered on the shores of the different bays, the smoke of their wigwams curled above the forest, and their canoes skimmed lightly over the waters; their song of praise might be heard at even-tide (for many of them, thanks to the heroic Catholic missionaries, were Christians, causing the woods to ring with melody. But the scene was changed when the fierce Iroquois burst like a destroying avalanche on the unsuspecting Hurons. Neither age nor sex was spared, the missionaries were burned at the stake, and only a miserable remnant of the Hurons escaped the rage of their enemies.

Arrived at either of these places mentioned, the traveller may embark on the commodious steamer belonging to the Muskoka and Nipissing Navigation Company, and taking the celebrated "Inner Channel," which Champlain followed in wonder and astonishment three hundred years ago, he will find himself in the midst of islands, on some of which the boat will almost touch; but just as his heart (if it is his first trip) is jumping into his mouth with fear, there is a turn of the wheel and the steamer's head falls gradually off and the danger is passed. Sometimes as she passes through a narrow channel you feel tempted to jump on the rock and take a run across one of the islands.

You can go right on to Parry Sound, where there is good hotel accommodation, and then by a good coach to the Muskoka Lakes, or if you are prepared to camp out the boat will stop to let you off wherever you wish.

In conclusion, allow me to say, "Give the islands of Georgian Bay one trial, the cost will not be much, and I am sure you will not regret it."

E. W. M.

PENETANGUISHENE, 1888.

## GEORGIAN BAY ; TO PARRY SOUND.

As the steamer glides down the bay of Penetanguishene the scenery is from the first beautiful and attractive. Green fields in other places reach down to the water's edge and in some places the dense forest stretches from the water up into the adjacent hills Near the entrance to the harbor on a commanding position stands the Reformatory, a Provincial institution, for juvenile offenders. The steamer usually goes by way of Midland on its way to Parry Sound.

Midland is comparatively a new place, and is beautifully situated on a rising ground running back from the waters of the harbor. There are several fine stores, hotels, and private residences. The town is making steady progress. The G. T. R. has a line into Midland, and large quantities of lumber and grain are shipped here.

Leaving Midland and proceeding northerly towards Parry Sound, the steamer soon enters the intricate channels of the island scenery of the north shore.

It is difficult to describe the marvellous beauty which meets the eye in all directions. It must be seen to be realized. It is without doubt among the most extensive and beautiful island scenery in the world.

Lying in or near the steamers course, between Penetanguishene and Parry Sound, there are about ten thousand islands of all sizes and shapes, some of them beautifully wooded and others almost bare rock, with sometimes only a few shrubs and trees. Channels stretch out in all directions, sometimes very narrow, at other times widening into beautiful bays. The steamer at times almost touches the shore as she glides through the narrow channels. At several points the tourist can get glimpses of the wide waters of the Georgian Bay while gliding through the sheltered channels of the steamer's course. Soon after leaving Penetanguishene the Giant's Tomb comes into view.

A LANDING PLACE.

This is a beautifully wooded island, and from whatever direction it is seen, seems to resemble an immense grave, hence its name, Giant's Tomb. Farther in the distance may be seen the three sisters of the Christian islands, Faith, Hope, and Charity. The largest of these, commonly called the Christian Island, was the scene of some of the most stirring events in the history of the unfortunate Huron nation.

The island is now inhabited by a band of Christian Indians of the Ojibway tribe. A few miles from Midland and Penetang. the tents and cottages of the island campers appear in sight, and nearly the whole trip to Parry Sound is enlivened by these health and pleasure seekers, their sail boats, row boats, and steam yachts gliding hither and thither in the placid waters.

The large number of the islands affords ample opportunity for an almost unlimited number of pleasure seekers to find pleasant spots to spend their summer vacation. Already hundreds have availed themselves of the unrivalled advantages of this region. These islands and the mainland adjoining have historic associations connected with the tragic history of the ill-fated Hurons. Hither a large number of them fled and took refuge from the savage ferocity of their implacable enemies the Iroquois. A bronze mortar of beautiful design was found near Parry Sound a few years ago bearing the date, cast in the metal, 1636, giving tangible proof of the truth of the thrilling events recorded by the Jesuit missionaries.*

As the steamer rounds the Moose Point the tourist is reminded that he is about half way between Parry Sound and Midland or Penetang. Old hunters tell the story of a fatal bear hunt which occurred near here some years ago.

An Indian had gone hunting, and not returning, search was made and he was found dead dreadfully torn, his gun and hunting-knife near his side. A dead bear not far distant with many wounds told the sad

---

* The relic (mortar) referred to, is in the possession of Wm. Beatty, Esq., Parry Sound.

tale of the deathly encounter. More recently near Kill Bear Point not far from Parry Sound an exciting and fatal bear fight took place in the water and for the truth of which the writer can vouch. One of the lumber tugs in passing through the channel at Kill Bear Point came near a large bear swimming across the channel. The men lowered their boat to try and capture it. Soon a boat manned by two lumbermen put out from the shore and gave chase. One of the men struck the bear a heavy blow with an axe, but the blow only wounded him. The bear immediately got into the boat and one of the men jumped into the water, the other man remaining in the stern of the boat. The bear made a rush for the man in the other end of the boat and a desperate encounter took place and the man jumped into the water and sank. His body was never found as the water was very deep at this place. The wounded bear swam to the shore and escaped before the men from the tug could overtake him.

As the steamer gets nearer Parry Sound the islands are generally more thickly wooded and beautiful, and some very narrow and picturesque channels are passed through. When about two miles distant the town of Parry Sound appears in sight, and the steamer enters the land-locked harbor—one of the safest and most commodious in the Dominion. Large saw-mills and immense piles of lumber tell the visitor that this is a lumber manufacturing centre.

Parry Sound is an incorporated town of nearly two thousand inhabitants and is growing steadily. The buildings are chiefly of wood, but several of them display good architectural taste. Prominent among the buildings which meet the eye of the visitor is the Belvidere Hotel, which occupies a beautiful and comanding position in the Belvidere Park. The view from the hotel in all directions is very charming, and the situation is such that there is almost always a cool breeze in the warm weather. This hotel has a high place in popular favour; the rooms are airy and clean, the meals good, and every reasonable attention paid to the guests. The hotel is only a short distance from the town, while it has all the beauty and retirement of the forest. Pleasant excursions can be made from Parry Sound either by land or water. The numerous islands and channels near Parry Sound afford an unusually good apportunity for boating, as the channels are safe, being sheltered from wind or sea. There is also good fishing in several places, for those fond of the sport. A very pleasant land excursion is the drive to McKellar. The scenery is beautifully diversified with lake and forest, and some new point of beauty meets the eye of the tourist at every turn. The drive from Perry Sound to Port Cockburn and Rosseau is also very attractive; the numerous lakes embosomed in the forest have a very pleasing effect. A daily stage connects Parry Sound with Port Cockburn and Rosseau. This gives tourists a choice of routes in visiting Parry Sound, and enables them to enjoy the beauties of the Muskoka Lakes as well as the magnificent scenery of the Georgian Bay. The M. & N. Navigation Co. have commodious and fast steamers in the Georgian Bay and the Muskoka Lakes.

The officers and employees of this line are obliging and attentive, and everything possible is done for the safety and comfort of passengers.

---

## WITH THE PRESS PARTY IN MUSKOKA.

Leaving here the party directed their steps towards Muskoka. Gravenhurst was reached early in the afternoon. A lively and picturesque scene is the wharf at this place at this season ; crowded with tourists coming and going, it at once points to the keen interest which this practically new route for health and pleasure seekers is awakening. The Muskoka and Nipissing Navigation Co., to whom the Press Association stands largely indebted for its courtesies, have a line of handsome and commodious boats plying on these waters. The accommodation offered is excellent and no better could possibly be desired. Leaving Gravenhurst the boat glides swiftly into lake Muskoka, a dark and sombre body of water, studded here and there with solemn and stately islands which are covered with trees of deepest green. These massive rocks rise abruptly from the depths of the lake and it is possible almost everywhere to run up to an island and find deep water without the service of wharf or pier. Innumerable tents and summer-houses are to be seen, and it is evident a large number of people are now in this retreat. Passing on to the head of Lake Muskoka, Port Carling is reached, where the night is passed. From this point boats run daily to Rosseau at the head of the beautiful lake of that name or to Port Cockburn at the head of Lake Joseph. Either of these lakes is a marvel of beauty in the way of scenery, are far different in their character from that of the lower lake. Handsome and substantial houses are to be found on many islands, and even elaborate residences which would do credit to a city avenue, are common. Altogether Muskoka is a place where few need seek rest and health in vain, and the happy cheerful faces which everywhere greet you in this district attest the fact that this is already recognized. We have no doubt that Muskoka will become very popular, and those of our readers who are looking for a few days' recreation or pleasure seeking we would heartily suggest a trip to this delightful locality so near at hand. The Press Party made a tour of the three lakes and enjoyed themselves immensely, returning from Rosseau on Saturday, making the trip in one and one-half days, from Gravenhurst.—*From the Beaverton Express.*

# "ALL ROUND TRIP."

MY DEAR MAUDE :—I would have answered your very welcome letter at an earlier date, but have just returned from a most enjoyable trip up North, and while away was too much absorbed in the scenery of the country, to think of writing.

We determined to conclude our pleasant holiday wanderings by taking—in the vernacular of The Muskoka Navigation Company—the "round trip." This is the tour of the Muskoka Lakes, from Gravenhurst to either Rosseau or Port Cockburn, then across to Parry Sound by stage, and from there down the Georgian Bay. Of course I went with uncle and aunt, and we started from Gravenhurst by an early boat, the "Kenosha," I think, arrived at Beamauris, we waited for the "Muskoka," which was to carry us into the upper lakes of Rosseau and Joseph.

When we were aboard and nicely settled in the bow, we began to really enjoy the scenery. We entered Lake Rosseau by Port Carling through the Indian River and in about half-an-hour found ourselves in a wilderness of pretty little islands. This, the Captain told us, is Venetia. It was about noon, and the sun shining brightly on the water, made the islands appear mammoth emeralds set in a sea of crispy wrinkled gold. It was a very brilliant scene—flags were flying from picturesque cottages and snowy tents ; hammocks were swinging in the groves, boats were swaying to and fro in their little bays and harbors, while their owners, in garbs so picturesque as in some instances to approach peculiarity, waved handkerchiefs with an energy and persistence that was truly wonderful.

We entered Lake Joseph by Port Sandfield and steered for Craigielea, we again entered Lake Joseph proper, and soon reached our destination,—Port Cockburn, at the head of the lakes. We had tea at Mr. Frasers' hotel, and I must say we found every-thing very nice indeed, wherever we went, whether on the steamers or at the hotels.

Next morning we were to begin the part of our round trip which interested me most. This was our journey by stage to Parry Sound. Our friends and others who knew our intentions had warned us that the drive would be fatiguing, but I was very anxious to go, and was not at all afraid of an eighteen-mile drive, even if the roads were rough. My greatest fear was that aunt would be dissuaded, and then of course I could not go. However, much to my relief, she declared herself quite determined, so we arranged to start in the morning.

The next day dawned beautifully, and after an early breakfast we started in high spirits. There were some Americans with us and an enthusiastic disciple of Isaak Walton who intended trying his luck by the shore of some solitary lake along the route.

We were rather crowded, but I really believe the Americans were glad as it afforded them an oppor-tunity of making innumerable jokes. There were some pails under the seats, and the driver advised us to put our feet into them, and so be more comfortable. The Americans with one accord accused each other of possessing pedal ornament on too extensive a scale, to admit of such stowing away.

ON LAKE ROSSEAU.

The road ran through woods to a great extent, and the trees kept the sun off us beautifully. The branches over-hung, and we could break them off with the greatest of ease, if our conveyance was not moving at too rapid a pace. The berry bushes and tall clumps of golden rod at the road side too, were almost within reach, and formed a hedge, gorgious in colour, on either side of us.

As the road is very hilly, we had a variety of scenery, and were continually rattling down into a cool green glade, and coming up on the other side at a slower pace. From the hill tops we saw glimpses of charming little lakes down in the valleys. They are nearly all named after some animal, native of the Dominion such as the Beaver, Deer, Bear, etc. The two finest, I believe, are named, Otter and Horseshoe Lakes.

I must not forget to tell you that the stage in which we travelled is facetiously called " in those parts," the " Jim Line." This line, owes its name to the fact that the *owner's* name is " Jim," the *driver's* name is " Jim," and the two stage horses are both named " Jim " also. We performed the historical feat of " Crossing the Boyne," indeed we crossed it twice; but unlike our royal predecessor, we were accommodated with a bridge each time. This small river is an-outlet of Otter Lake, and is a most picturesque stream, winding erratically along the bottom of a valley. As we approached the Georgian Bay, or, more properly speaking, the Sound, the air grew deliciously cool and breezy, and about noon we caught sight of the water, and entered first Parry Harbor, then Parry Sound, and finally the Belvidere hotel, our destination for the time being. We were very little tired by our journey, and were delighted that we had undertaken it. It is intended immediately, I believe, to make the road smoother and also to have better stage accommodation ; but we did not fare so badly after all. We were very much pleased with our hotel. It is spacious, kept in the nicest order, and above all has a delightful situation. We wandered about the grounds, wooded with young oaks, and sloping to the beach, and then went to inspect the town. We stayed over at the Belvidere, and one morning went aboard the "Maxwell," for Penetanguishene and Midland.

The "Northern Belle" and "Telegram" were in the harbor with a regular fleet of smaller boats, pleasure yachts and tugs, forming altogether a very animated scene. We were off quite early, and found the morning air fresh and delightful. The scenery is very fine, and the tiny rocky islets, scarcely showing above the water, were objects of our particular interest. These "submerged peaks," would, I am sure, prove a very interesting study for a geologist. The bay was quite rough enough, I thought, although the "Maxwell's" course lies through the deservedly famed inside channel. We saw glimpses between the islands of the outer route and of Lake Huron, and the waves appeared alarmingly high. Now and then we noticed a large sailing yacht, out in the lake, so far away that it looked like a white bird, then a cloud of dark smoke indicated the course of some steamer making its way through the rough water. We also saw the rock on which the "Wabuno" was wrecked and which is marked by a derrick. The islands range from about a yard square of rock, to fine well-wooded ones, such as Parry Island and seem almost innumerable. We counted nearly one hundred that could be seen from the steamer, at a single glance around. What I like particularly about the tiny islands along our course is, that the waves break against them in showers of spray and gives them the appearance of a shoal of miniature whales disporting themselves in the sun.

We reached the town of Penetanguishene about one o'clock p.m., and after a short stay the " Maxwell " proceeded to Midland. There we left her with sincere regrets and feeling that we had all too soon completed the " Round Trip."

With love to all, yours affectionately,

DOLLY, *Port Hope.*

---

EXTRACT FROM THE " CANADA PRESBYTERIAN."

Muskoka and Georgian Bay are the breathing places and play-grounds for Western Ontario. Muskoka being the right lung. When you enter Muskoka from the south the Northern Railway puts you down at Gravenhurst. The central figure on the platform during the season is A. P. Cockburn. Mr. Cockburn is not a man of many words, he does not " gush " and call you " dear brother " or any of that kind; but when you go aboard one of his trim boats you find clergymen travel for half-fare. That pleases you immensely. Leaving Gravenhurst you go

ded ones,
merable.
be seen
What I
our course
owers of
shoal of
sun.
bout one
ell" pro-
sincere
mpleted

*Hope.*

IAN."

eathing
Mus-
uskoka
u down
latform
Cock-
es not
of that
n boats
That
you go

to dinner, and if there is any half-fare about that part of the business the fault will be your own. From Gravenhurst to Rosseau or Port Cockburn the scenery for quiet beauty is unsurpassed in America. There is nothing of its kind anywhere that surpasses Lake Joseph. One of the best things about Muskoka is that when there you see a large number of your friends. The distances are not great and as there are thousands of tourists, you meet somebody every hour that you are pleased to meet. The left lung of Ontario consists of the Georgian Bay. The trip acoss the Georgian Bay is one of the most bracing and health-giving in America ; a tired man can find rest and cool breezes at a slight cost. All any one needs to find a good play-ground is a little time, a little money and a little common sense.

Among the many things that we should be thankful for in Canada are the many inviting and healthful spots where weary workers can find recreation and rest.

P.S.—The contributor has no pass on any line of steamers. This is a source of deep regret to him at present and may be some reason why he does not give any particular line a " puff." Had he a pass like some of his brethren of the quill, he might be able to tell the readers of the *Presbyterian* what line they should go by. A pass throws great light on that subject. As an educator a pass is a great success.

EXTRACT FROM A LETTER BY MR. J. R. TENNANT,
OF RICHWOOD. '

" The numerous islands in Lakes Muskoka and
Rosseau and the shores and islands of a great many
of the smaller lakes affords excellent opportunities for
camping parties, and for healthfulness Muskoka cannot be surpassed by any region in Canada. I have
known asthmatic persons (who had at times great
difficulty in breathing while at home in the southern
counties of Ontario) to be entirely free from their
troubles while living in Muskoka. Bear, deer and
duck shooting is very good. The lakes and creeks
are teeming with fish which may be caught by any
novice in their proper season. There are plenty of
deer in every section I have visited.

" Muskoka, which a few years ago was the habita-
tion of the Indian and the lumberman, has developed
into a charming and popular summer resort, to which
people flock from all parts of the continent to enjoy
the beauty of the scenery, and escape the heat and
dust of the city. The extension of the Northern railway to Gravenhurst has enabled the tourist to reach
the first of the chain of lakes, over which the elegant
steamers of the Muskoka and Nipissing Navigation
Co. will carry him in comfort and safety to any desired
destination. It is estimated that during the season
just closing not less than 25,000 persons have visited
this district."

## WHAT THE BRITISH SCIENTISTS HAVE TO SAY ABOUT MUSKOKA.

" Of the enjoyment which we derived from our short excursion to Muskoka it would be difficult to speak in too high terms. The railway journey through the cultivated parts gave us a good idea of your settled districts, while the gradual transition to the unsettled which we passed through on our journey here, showed us, as it were, an epitome of your short history. The beauty of the sail through the Muskoka Lakes, filled us with astonishment and delight, and will long live in our memories. We have no scenery of this kind in our own country, and those of us who have seen the famous Thousand Islands of the St. Lawrence, prefer the Muskoka Lakes thereto; moreover, the rest and quiet communion with nature, which we have thus enjoyed, has been most grateful to those of us who, having taken a more or less active part in the meetings of the Association at Montreal, came to Toronto somewhat wearied both in body and mind."

---

## THE OPINION OF A MEDICAL GENTLEMAN.

DR. D. J. GRANT, now of Gravenhurst, who has practised for many years in the older parts of the Province, speaks in the highest terms of the health giving and invigorating qualities of the Muskoka Territory. He says:—" Not only is its diversity of pine-clad hill and dale refreshing, both to mind and body, but its magnificent stretches of soft water and the remarkable purity of its atmosphere, its altitude being several hundred feet above that of Lake Ontario, render it specially beneficial to those labouring under diseases of the mucuous membranes, such as Bronchitis, Asthma, Kidney affections, etc." The Doctor also speaks of the benefits he has derived personally, and many others who have come under his notice and advice have given similar testimonies.

----

## "HAY FEVER."

STEUBENVILLE, Ohio, 19th April, 1888.

EDWARD PROWSE, ESQ., Beaumaris, Muskoka.

MY DEAR SIR,—In reply to your enquiry of the 16th inst.,

In the past seven years my son, Charles has spent the hay-fever season, the months of August and September at Macinac, Mich., Marquette, Mich., Oakland, Ind., Chautauqua, N. Y., and Beaumaris, Muskoka. Two seasons each at Mackinac, Oakland and Muskoka. He suffers more from hay-fever than any one of my acquaintance and was benefited at each of these places, but at none of them did he enjoy entire immunity from the disease, except at Beaumaris.

Judging from his experience I consider Beaumaris the best place for hay-fever patients to go. I may also add that he found the other attractions of Beaumaris more to his liking than any of the others.

In this latter view I can heartily join with him, having myself participated in it. ·

I remain, Yours truly,

(Signed), CHARLES GALLAGHER.

---

ST. CATHARINES, ONT., 4th April, 1888.

EDWARD PROWSE, ESQ., Beaumaris.

DEAR SIR,—I have suffered from hay-fever for many years, about twenty, and for two seasons enjoyed perfect freedom from this trying disease at your well-kept and charmingly situated hotel.

Yours truly,

(Signed), THOS. R. MERRITT.

---

EXTRACTS FROM LETTER WRITTEN BY MR. JAS. DALTON, OF CINCINNATI, O.

" These chains of lakes are unlike any other of our inland lakes, and possess the most beautiful and grand scenery of any water on the continent. The scenery is even more beautiful than that of the Thousand Islands of the St. Lawrence River, which is considered the finest in America. We pass up through a beautiful sheet of water clear as crystal and smooth as a mirror reflecting the islands. As you glide along you hear on every side exclamations from the party: 'How grand! how beautiful!' ROSSEAU—We found the air health-giving and our appetites good for breakfast, after which we took a boat to explore Shadow River, where the water is so clear that the trees and objects are reflected to a great depth. There is fine boating and fine fishing at Port Carling. BEAUMARIS —The best fishing ground to be found anywhere ; we experienced for new beginners at the art, fine success. Bass is found here from one to five pounds, and hauls are made from 35 to 100 pounds in from two to three hours fishing. A party of hunters took in thirty-two deer in fifteen days. Bear is to be seen almost any season of the year."

---

PHILADELPHIA ENQUIRER SAYS.

"All who have visited these charming regions will agree with what these several writers say of the lakes— Muskoka, Rosseau and Joseph. The ride by steamer through these lakes, unoppressed by heat, is simply charming."

## AT BURK'S FALLS.

How well I can recall that pleasant week, my first in the district of Magnetawan. Muskoka is as familiar and as delightful to me as to any of its devotees, who annually resort there to repair their shattered health, or ease their overtaxed minds in its beneficial dissipations. But Magnetawan broke upon my vision in all its enchanting novelty, and more than repaid me for my extended journey.

One may proceed direct from Gravenhurst by the Northern Pacific Junction Railway to Burk's Falls, one of the best summer resorts in Ontario for lovers of fishing ; but our party, after a tour on the Lakes of Muskoka, left the Navigation Company's steamer at Bracebridge, and from there travelled by that line of railway to Burk's Falls. By this means, we had a few hours to spare in Bracebridge, and employed them in inspecting that rapidly increasing town.

I suppose the Northern Pacific Junction Railway is but a very small edition of the great C. P. R. ; but to my limited experience it seemed grand enough. I was never weary of staring from the car window, and speculating about the amount of labour and earth it took to construct its immense elevation. The line is a little over one hundred miles in length and is most uniformly level, though running through a most mountainous country, depressed by valleys and intersected with rivers. It is remarkable for the number of trestle bridges necessary in making it direct, the Magnetawan river alone being crossed no less than four times.

It was almost five o'clock in the afternoon when we left Bracebridge, the train being late, and shortly after seven o'clock Burk's Falls was reached. Never shall I forget my first view of that interesting place. It was a lovely evening in the latter end of June, and the fresh, sweet air of that northerly district was doubly grateful after the heat and dust of an afternoon spent in the train.

Mr. Menzies, the agent of the Muskoka and Nipissing Navigation Company, met us at the station, as we were expected, and accompanied us to the " Burk House." During our whole visit to Burk's Falls and its vicinity, Mr. Menzies showed us every attention, pointing out objects of interest, explaining complicated matters, and entertaining us with amusing local anecdotes, in which art he pre-eminently excels.

Having heard most favourable comments upon the accommodation of " The Burk House," we determined to make it our head-quarters, projecting our excursions in all directions from that point. We accordingly drove there from the station, through little woods and amongst the hills. It was an enchanting drive, just long enough, and exhilarating enough to make us all feel our merriest, and on the best of terms with all the world. We could not forbear smiling continually, and occasionally grasping the back of the seats when bounding over the undulating road.

At length we were set down at our chosen hotel, and received most hospitably by mine host, who is a gentleman to be noticed anywhere. He suggests some of Thackeray's heroes to the mind, and oh! that Dickens or Thackeray were here to do justice to adventures through which we passed. None but Dickens could describe the *recherché* supper served in the dining-room of the old hotel, that of the new building just being completed at the time of our visit.

ON THE GEORGIAN BAY BY MOONLIGHT.

I think it was one of the pleasantest modes of proceeding to a *salle à manger*, certainly a most novel one. Imagine us descending the front steps of the grand hotel, and promenading in the pine-scented air a few paces down the street to a charmingly old-fashioned dwelling. But if it were pleasant to repair there in the evening, how much was the enjoyment enhanced, where the visit was repeated in the early morning, when the dew was on the grass. The fresh air and the delicate viands would have brought an appetite to the most debilitated invalid.

Though Burk's Falls was found little more than ten years ago, it is a place of considerable importance; it seems as if ten years with Burk's Falls was as an hundred years with most other places. Besides the " Burk House " there are two other very large hotels, "The Cataract" and " The Clifton." Not having been inside these last, I cannot say more than that their situations are pleasant, and their outsides preposessing. As for the new " Burk House," it boasts of new and fashionable furniture and all modern conveniences, including electric bells communicating with every apartment. The village has a complete telephone system, is well stocked with stores and business places, and of course has a postoffice and a telegraph office.

Desiring to see as much as possible, we walked through the village that same evening and inspected all objects of interest. The road to the wharf was most picturesque; bordered with trees, ferns and wild flowers, and here and there a spring of clear cold water trickled from the high bank on one side of the road. In full view of the steamer at her mooring are falls and rapids, where some mills have been built advantageously.

One never seems to tire of walking in the calm of a village evening, where the views are new and pleasing, and utterly devoid of the excitement of city sight-

seeing. Here authors repair to empty their teeming
brains in peaceful solitude; here Canada's most accomplished divines find ease from grinding brain
labour; and here is the fisherman's paradise. We
were not a sporting party, our enjoyment consisted of
much the same order as the lilies of the field, breathing the fresh air, basking in the sunshine, and as free
from care as is possible on this earth. That summer
evening's walk will always be remembered as one of
the brightest and pleasantest of my life.

We had long heard of the famous, very much twisted
Magnetawan River, and indeed that was the object we
had travelled so far to see. So next morning we embarked on the steamer *Wenonah*, Capt. Kennedy, a
courteous and efficient navigator. This vessel is
unique, it being, I am told, the only paddle and screw
steamer on the continent. It was a little idea of the
manager, and is as successful as its sanguine projector
could wish it to be. In parts of the river paddle
wheels only can be used, in others again the screw
alone can avail, and when both modes of progression
are employed the progress is most rapid.

I wonder is there another river so winding in the
world, and yet blessed with regular steamers. The
most careful steering is necessary on the river, and the
present wheelmen are extraordinary expert. It must
have been very enlivening one former season when the
unskilful pilot went crashing into one bank, then into
the other. The land appears to be level along the
river, and very fertile and well cultivated. At Ballam's Landing, where the boat took on wood, some
exquisite garden strawberries were brought on board.

These were served for early dinner in their natural state and excelled any I ever saw for sale in cities.

Along the river's banks grew sweet wild-roses, and the boats stopping at settlers' wharves enabled us to gather them.

We had half-an-hour to see Magnetawan village, quite a flourishing little place. It has been remarked of Muskoka that flowers are cultivated under every circumstance, in every place and by every dweller there. The same may be said of this district. We were presented with most beautiful crimson roses with velvety petals, perfumed, and of a very large variety. Wherever we went we met with unvarying kindness and honest politeness. The scenery along the Magnetawan is beautiful; the shore is thickly wooded and the river so narrow that one can almost reach the branches of the trees from the boat. Monotony is escaped in the widening of the river into lakes, from three to six miles wide, notably among which are " Cecebe" or Duck Lake, "Ahmic" or Beaver Lake. Navigation terminates at Ahmic Harbour, and this is "the place to fish," *par excellence.* Here two of our friends in part of an afternoon caught between sixty and seventy bass, some of them being very large.

We, who did not go for fishing, returned to Burk's Falls that same day. The whole trip, including return, occupied twelve most enjoyable hours. We had late dinner before leaving the boat and, trivial as it may seem to many, I must mention an article of the repast —it was the nicest pie any of us had ever tasted in our whole existence—made from some of the strawberries taken on board at Ballam's Landing on the way down. I must cut short the recounting of our adventures and merely relate how we got back from this comparatively unknown land. The Northern Pacific Junction Railway connecting with the C. P. R. at North Bay, passes Burk's Falls between ten and eleven p.m., with its passengers from Winnipeg and the far west for Toronto. There are of course daily trains, but this is the most popular one, as no time is lost by taking it. We steal, as it were, the hours of night, being carried swiftly forward while asleep and wake up at Toronto.

We left Burk's Falls with hopes of seeing it again, and with the firm determination to persuade all our friends to repair there as quickly as possible.

M.

---

MY DEAR MARY:—As Spring is a good time to make plans for summer travelling, I want to tell you of a trip I took last summer, in fact I went three times ; but a description of one of the trips will suffice, and perhaps I may persuade you to come, and see all its beauties for yourself. Our trip was to Parry Sound, on the *Maxwell*, through the Georgian Bay Islands, of which there are eight thousand in this bay alone. I suppose I had better begin telling of this especial journey from the very beginning. Well then, having made up a nice little party, we all started for the wharf where the *Maxwell* lay moored. We had not far to go, because we were already in Penetanguishene. Having got all our belongings together we stepped on board, and of course, as we had engaged two cabins we instantly looked them up. (By-the-by, there are only four altogether for passengers, the boat not being intended to have accommodation of that description.) We found two neat-looking rooms, small certainly, but snug, and quite big enough. Here we left our wraps, which we had not packed up in our trunks, because we thought we should need them before the day was over, and very glad were we that we were so provided, because the mornings and evenings are cool on the water, not to say cold, and an ulster or shawl is most comfortable, and enables one to stay out in the air, when otherwise one would be obliged to retire to the saloon. On deck we speedily settled ourselves, but the sun poured down, and we were obliged to hunt around for a cool place, where we could still watch for any passengers that might come. The *Maxwell* waits for the train from Toronto to come in, and we were not seated very long before we saw the business-like train come in, and stop at the station a short distance off. Then when her work there was done, the tinkle, tinkle, of the bell sounded, and we saw her slowly coming our way, until she stopped right in front of the *Maxwell.* Sometimes when the train is late, the *Maxwell* after going to Midland, returns to Penetanguishene for passengers or freight. Time being up, off we start, and no one is alive for sights. First we notice the pretty town, with its houses on the hill, and as our eyes travel down, we see the usual amount of boathouses and lumber, by the shore. Now being well under way, and going quickly, we have only time to notice that the opposite shore is thickly wooded, with spaces here and there, which gives it a park-like look ; then to have

Mr. Davidson's lumber mill pointed out, and Mr. Beck's on the town side, also the tannery. Proudly the *Maxwell* like a stately swan, passes pretty little Magazine Island on the right, where the powder was kept in 1812, and where between it, and the Reformatory shore, we would see if we hunted around in a small boat, the hull of an old oak English gun boat, sunk about that time. It was once to be partly seen above water, but relic seekers have diminished its dimensions. There is another in the North-West Basin. There was once an old military store house, on the Reformatory shore, opposite to Magazine Island, but it has long since disappeared. The tiny house on Magazine Island is the only remnant left to remind us of those warlike times, and many a modern name is cut or penceled on its wooden walls. Now we pass the Superintendent's picturesque house on the hill, nestling amongst the trees, with the Deputy-Superintendent's pretty domicile in close proximity. Then comes the Reformatory for Boys, which looks quite imposing. Now past the chaplain's house, then by what was at one time the officers old quarters, on we go past the breakwater next, with its lighthouse, and on the left, after a few minutes, we sweep by Whiskey Island, so called because the Indians, at one time, I am told, used to stop here, to drink their "fire water" which they had purchased in Penetanguishene. It was once an island with trees on it, but there is nothing left now except a small rock on which there has been a lighthouse placed. The scenery beginning now to be uninteresting, out come our books, and we are soon interested in fiction, nor do we see much in the landscape after this to attract, until we enter a smiling bay, and perceive we are arriving at Midland City, a busy ambitious little place. Here we get our letters and papers, having left orders for them to be forwarded by stage, and the boy politely brings them on board to us. Off again, and somewhere near three o'clock we again get a glimpse of the Reformatory in the distance, as we skirt along Beau Soleil Island. Nothing much to be seen now but broad expanse of water, and very distant islands, but about five o'clock or perhaps a little later, we wake up from our books, with a thrill of delight, for we are entering the place where the islands are closer together, so no more books are needed to beguile the time, there is enough now to keep eyes and mind employed. The air is so fresh and sweet, the heavens, water, and earth seem agreed in trying to charm, alas! pen can never adequately describe all there is to see, and it would take a very clever brush to picture the beauty all around us, or even a tithe of it. The soul can only drink it in till the noblest part of one's nature is aroused to full appreciation, and a feeling of adoration rises to the Mighty Creator of it all. So close do we come to some of the islands, that you feel sure you must touch, but no, safely onward we go. Now we see nothing but an island before us, outlet there is none to be seen, surely we are not going to run on shore! involuntarily you hold your breath, then surely and steadily you see the *Maxwell* like a living thing. turn to the right, where lies revealed a beautiful little channel, not seen before. On we go past a perky little tug, as proudly passing it we almost look down its funnel. On still on, till we come to the " Narrows " where we lessen speed, going very slowly, for there are treacherous rocks hidden below on the left side. It looks about sixty feet wide, and as the *Maxwell* is forty feet in width, there does not seem to be much room to spare, but I heard that men worked there during the day, making it wider for vessels passing through. It begins to be too dark now to see much more of the scenery, but night has its own beauty, the stars brightly shine reflecting their rays in the water below. Grand Orion with his bright belt, Casiopia's chair, the big and little Dippers, and the mysterious North Star, etc. Still on in and out between islands, one is lost in admiration of the beautiful steering, what a keen sight, calm nerve, and steady strong arm is needed here. At last we are moored about nine o'clock, and very sorry are we to leave such a nice snug boat, though on arriving at the Belvidere Hotel we find it very comfortable, and its host most attentive. Our journey through such sweet fresh air, soon makes us long for bed, which after a cosy chat, we speedily seek, and Morpheus lends his aid in mixing up visions of fairy land, with the scenes we have gone through. The next day being Sunday, we repair to the English Church, where we enjoy the service, especially the music which is a surprising treat. There are other churches here of other denominations, so no one need feel at a loss in that respect. Parry Sound is a quiet place, but very pretty, I am not going to tell you too much about it, for you must come and see it for yourself. Back we go to the *Maxwell* on Sunday night, so that we need not get up too early in the morning. The *Maxwell* starts about a quarter to six, and that is soon enough for pleasure seekers. We regretted we could not stay longer in Parry Sound but having made arrangements to be home at a certain date, we were obliged to go. Now the morning scenery must be seen to be really enjoyed. It is superb! We could hardly eat our breakfasts, so anxious were we not to lose any pretty sight, and many a run did we take for a look, bound to let nothing beautiful escape us. The shadows are so deep, every island reflected as if in a mirror, and the morning air is so delicious, that you feel as if you could, like Tennyson's brook, "go on forever." Now if you are tired of city life, and your father and brothers want to have the cobwebs swept out of their brains, come and see this inland passage, and stay for a short time at Parry Sound, you will go home invigorated and brightened, and will feel that it is good to have taken the trip. The Captain and Purser are both most kind Many people buy islands, where they camp for the summer, and their fires form a romantic sight at night. The *Maxwell* leaves Penetang about one o'clock p.m.

Your affectionate,

ALTHEA.

# A SPECIMEN MUSKOKA LETTER.

DEAR TOM :—I wrote you last on my arrival at Toronto, and not caring to spend the balance of my holidays in a city, made up my mind to put in the last week in the far-famed Muskoka Lakes ; so went down to Mr. Barlow Cumberland's office on Yonge St., and purchased a ticket for Beaumaris. Off next morning at 8 a.m., per Northern Ry. for Gravenhurst, where I arrived about 1.30. I found a very comfortable steamer waiting to take us up the lakes ; had dinner which was served on the boat in first-rate style, and, after about an hour and a-half sail up the lake, found myself at Beaumaris. Here I found a first-rate hotel with capital accommodation. Having secured my room, I took a walk around the place to inspect my new quarters. There is a most beautiful view from the front of the house, and a balmy breeze from across the lake, was most enjoyable. Some guests were playing tennis on the fine lawn in front, and I purpose putting in part of my time in the same way. I then looked up my fishing tackle, and got things in order for the next day. Had supper about half past six, then got a boat and took an hour's row to get myself in training. After, returned to the hotel where I found the folks dancing. There is a large room here which is always ready for that or any like purpose. Next morning, having had lunch put up for me, I started off with a guide for a day's fishing, and commencing just below the hotel, fished along

6

the shores of the island, casting in at all likely spots, and so went on till noon with a result of ten nice bass and three pickerel. We landed at a pretty point, made a fire, got some coffee, cooked sufficient fish for dinner, and I can tell you that is the way to enjoy them, right fresh out of the water into the frying-pan; I never tasted anything like it before. About half-past three we started again, returning to the hotel for supper, with a grand result of thirty-two bass and several pickerel— not so bad for one day. In the evening played billiards. Next morning, about 9 a.m., the steamer called here, on her way to Bala, the out-let of these waters, so I took a trip on her. We first went up to Point Kaye P.O. and left the mails, then across to Bala, where we arrived about 10.30. It is a most beautiful spot. There is a fine waterfall, also a large dam where all the logs go over into the river below. Arrived back at the hotel in time for dinner. This is a splendid trip; the scenery all along the route is simply magnificent. I put in the afternoon playing lawn tennis and bathing: in the evening there was lots of good music and singing.

Next day, after my morning bath I rowed over to Huckleberry Rock, a place about two miles distant, although only about a mile as the crow flies. It gets its name from the quantity of berries growing upon it, and certainly there is any quantity of them. I climbed to the top of the rock and walked several hundred yards, to place called the Lookout, and here I got one of the finest views I think I ever saw. Nearly the whole of Muskoka Lake and part of Lake Rosseau lay before me, with the islands dotted here and there; it was a perfect panorama. I returned to the hotel for dinner. In the afternoon I played lawn tennis for a while, and then went down to the bowling-alley for an hour; in the evening had a good dance.

Next day, I and some others took a ramble through the woods as far as Leonard Lake, a very pretty lake about two miles from here. On the way gathered any amount of wild raspberries, also got a lot of pitcher plants. I had never seen any before; they are very pretty and peculiar. Put in the rest of the day playing billiards and bathing. Next day I spent fishing with pretty much the same result as before. In the evening there was a concert in the dancing-room, which went off very well. Sunday, there was service in the morning and afternoon; in the evening most of the guests assembled in the music-room and had selections of sacred music, sang hymns, etc. On Monday, the proprietor having engaged a steam-boat for the day, about fifty guests took a trip up to the head of lakes Rosseau and Joseph, stopping about an hour at each place. This was truly a delightful sail; we saw everything at the best advantage and enjoyed the day thoroughly, getting back to the hotel about 7 p.m., when we found our supper ready for us. I am spending this evening writing you, as I think it is the best opportunity I shall have, as I must get away to-morrow morning. I only wish I could stay here for a month, as I feel twenty per cent. better since I came, and have gained about five pounds in weight. The air is so good and cool I always sleep well at nights, and as for appetite I am afraid to think of it; I am sure the landlord made very little out of me. I hear several people who have suffered for years from hay fever, say they have never been so well anywhere as here. In fact they have been quite free from it. Now I must close, as I am sure you will be getting tired, and all I can say is that if you want to enjoy yourself and have a real good time, go to Muskoka and spend a week or two. Yours,

BOB.

---

## MIDLAND.

PRETTILY situated with rising ground on either side and in the rear lies the ambitious little town of Midland with the main street running down to the commodious steamboat docks. Midland has grown with the rapidity of a Western States town and has now a population of over 2000. On its principal business street several fine brick blocks have been erected showing evidences of stability which speak well for its assured future. It is fast attaining eminence as the lumber town of Canada, having now several lumber shingle and planing mills, while immense quantities of lumber brought from mills built up the north shore are handled from vessels to cars and distributed through Ontario and the Eastern States. The grain trade between Chicago, Duluth and other points with Midland is extensive, the capabilities of the Midland elevator being equal to any on the lakes, and so satisfactory has been this branch of the Company's business that the Grand Trunk are contemplating the erection of a second elevator. With splendid hotel accommodation yachting, etc., Midland is a desirable " stopping over " point for the tourist after doing the beauties of the Georgian Bay.

# HINTS AS TO CAMPING OUTFIT.

THE opinions of campers differ as to the tent equip-
ments, the more fastidious choosing some articles
scorned by those who despise luxury in camp or object
to the trouble of conveying extra furniture. However to
novices in the art of campers the following lists may
be acceptable, being the most necessary requirements :

Equipment—Ridge tent, No. 3. The pole can be
carried from place to place and the pins and uprights
cut on landing. A large party will find that the provision of a tent for the food supply and cooking will
not be regretted. Axe, hatchet, deep pot or bake
kettle, sauce pan, frying pan, gridiron, kettle, teapot
long iron spoon, long iron fork, butcher's knife, knives,
forks and spoons, tin washdish, round tin dishpans,
tin cups, tin or thick earthenware plates, water pail,
sugar, salt, pepper, and tea cans, matches, sperm
candles, two hand lanterns for candles.

PROVISIONS—Biscuits, flour, bread, sides clear bacon
sewn in canvas, tea, sugar, salt, pepper, soap in bars,
condensed milk, raisins, beans, dried apples, rice, lime
juice or lemons.

CLOTHING—One change of underclothing, flannel
shirt and woollen trousers ; three or four pairs of wool
socks, overcoat or mackintosh, heavy long boots for
day, pair easy old gaiter boots or leather slippers for
camp, extra cap or tuque, handy bag for small things,
large dunnage bag to hold all clothing.

Ladies require one change of underclothing, several
pairs of woollen stockings, waterproof cloak, a jacket

for chilly evenings, stout boots for walking outdoors, and shoes or slippers in camp, they also may have an extra toque and handy bag for small articles. But two dresses are necessary, one for travelling from home to the camp and return, and a serge or thin flannel of dark colour to wear about the camp. A bathing suit completes the list.

---

## HINTS TO CAMPING PARTIES.

IF the party consists of over six, they should club together and hire a cook, probably a son of Shem This will enable all hands to be on their feet from morning till night, and that is the reason why camping out is so healthful—you take fifteen times as much exercise in camp as you take in your city life. You get up about half-past four or five and are out on the deer trail or casting the fly before six. There are no lights in the camp, for when nine o'clock comes all hands are sound asleep on their mattresss of pine boughs. By the dawn of the day all hands are thoroughly rested and ready for another hard trot over hill and dale, with rifle or rod in hand. But if the party is less than six, one of the crowd should do the cooking, with the understanding that the others should take turns in washing the dishes for him, The labour of a camp can be divided up very evenly in this way and nobody be the worse for it. The question with most campers is, what to do with their large fish. Small trout are always nice when fried, but big hunks of fried trout are not so acceptable. To overcome this difficulty, let me suggest that you fry your small fish and boil your large ones or "shingle" them. And as there is many a camper who has never eaten "shingled trout," let me give the mode of operation. Take a shingle and bore a hole about half an inch at the thin end. Into this insert the end of a stick about sixteen inches long. Take a trout from fourteen to sixteen inches long, split him down the back and tack him to the shingle so as to spread him well apart. Wait till the fire burns down so that it ceases to smoke, and then set your shingle up before it so that as you butter the head of the trout it will run down all through the meat. Put on salt and pepper when you take the fish off your shingle, and you will agree with me that it is a very toothsome morsel. For a boiled fish you merely require a sauce of milk and butter, thickened with bread crumbs.

Venison should be another standard article of food in the camp : and the man who cannot eat it at least twice a day has no relish for outdoor life. Not an ounce of a deer's flesh should be allowed to go to waste The bones will furnish you a delicious soup ; the head can be baked under the ashes till you ask if the deer had two heads, so palatable does it seem. You can fry the liver and heart with rashers of bacon, and the ribs—well, they should be roasted over the coals.

Don't think of going out without a tent if you calculate to stay longer than three days ; and don't take white blankets, for gray are preferable and the chocolate colour still better. Pitch your tent a short distance from the lake or river, and about twenty yards farther down fix your camp table and kitchen, so that the flies will not come about the place where you sleep. Lop off fir boughs and lay them on the ground at least a foot deep before you spread your blankets on them. In starting for camp get a box at least 5 x 3 feet and divide it off into at least three compartments, into one of which pack your ironware and nail down securely. This box you can hang up endways when you reach camp, and it will serve you as a cupboard. Remember, too, that each man should take his day as camp-keeper. No well-regulated camp is ever to be left wholly alone. Some neighboring campers may be in need of something you can spare as well as not; and yet, on arriving at your camp, and finding no one there, be deterred from touching anything, no matter how trifling its value; and remember, also, that you are at all times liable to be in need of similar accommodations. Nor must you forget to take along a little box of needles and thread, for the cat briars will tear your clothes, and you should mend them thoroughly before starting out again.

A word as to clothing may not be amiss at this time. Wear what you like on your journey to and from camp, for there is no need of your coming back to town looking like a ragamuffin. But take all your old clothes to camp and wear them out. If you will show me a man who has to have a suit made expressly for fishing, I will show you a fellow who is an indifferent companion in the woods. Your thoroughbred woodman is a man who goes out for rest and repose of mind, which is so easily gained by a moderate fatigue of the body. Such a man aims at the greatest amount of comfort with the least possible

expense. He shows his qualifications for woodland
life by the way he-keeps his camp cleanly, by the
whiteness of his dishes and the tidy appearance of his
tent inside. He will show it also in his dignity of
behaviour, remembering that a tent on the lakeshore is
just as fitting a place for the display of good breed-
ing as the ball-room or the counting-house. The
man who thinks he can behave unseemly because he
is in camp and there is nobody but his camp-fellows
to see him, is a very good man to leave behind on the
next trip. My word for it, there is no place to judge
of men like a woodland camp for hunting and fishing.
If a man has a mean streak in him it will surely come
out then—G. M.

## BRACEBRIDGE

Is an important official and business centre, situated
at the head of navigation on Muskoka River, six miles
from the lake. The village, with a population of 750,
was incorporated in 1875, under a by-law of the County
Council of Victoria. Present population about 1,500.
There are a large number of dry goods, clothing, gro-
cery and provision stores here, besides three hardware
gunsmiths, three book, periodical and fancy goods, and
three drug stores, three law firms, two medical doctors,
two newspaper offices, a large tannery, four saw mills,
a large wood-working establishment, etc. The place
is centrally situated in the judicial and territorial district of Muskoka, on the line of the Q. P. J. Railway,
ten miles north of the town of Gravenhurst, and can
thus be reached by rail or water. We refer to the

business standing of Bracebridge so that tourists and sportsmen may not encumber themselves with supplies which can be obtained here.

Mr. W. E. Hamilton, B.A., writing in the *Muskoka Atlas*, says :—" Bracebridge is eminently the natural centre for tourists who wish to see the Muskoka water-falls with a minimum expenditure of time and money. * * * Not the least attractive cascade (60 feet in descent) is in the heart of the village. Standing on the bridge which spans the cataract, the tourist scans at one glance the Bracebridge Fall, and the two dark and smooth bodies of water which precede and follow it. On one side of the bridge the placid and unrippled water plows under a lofty and curving plateau covered with villas, sloping down near the bridge to a little germ of green prairie, darkened by the shade of over-hanging pines. * * * Turning from this glimpse of lake-like placidity, let the tourist step to the south-western hand-rail of the bridge, and find a tranforma-tion effected. Glassy stillness and gloomy darkness of water are succeeded by white sparkling foam, and the turmoil of the petted element, in all its tempestuous loveliness. Water in every conceivable shape and contraction is here, sometimes thundering over some jutting craft which has defied its power from century to century, or again striking against a hidden splinter of gneiss, and thowing up a fountain of foam and spray to sparkle in the summer sun." Since the ex-tract taken from the ready pen of Mr. Hamilton was written, the railway bridge has been constructed over the river at the Fall.

The High Fall is on the north branch four miles

from Bracebridge, and the beautiful Muskoka Fall, on the south branch, three miles distant. Mr. Hamilton gives his first impressions of his visit to this Fall :— " The traveller comes on the cataract unaware. He is driving along a comparatively level road, with nothing whatever to suggest cataracts in the surrounding scenery, when suddenly he pulls up at the South Falls bridge, and the raging scene of boiling waters almost takes away his breath. Deafened by their thunder, dazzled their uprising spray, composed by the suddenness of the apparition, he gladly turns to collect his thoughts, towards the upper portion of the river." The South Falls is a favorite resort for picnic parties from Bracebridge, who go up the south branch a distance of four miles, in row-boats or canoes. On the hottest days the spray, the foaming waters, makes the immediate surroundings cool. There is a beautiful fresh-water spring and a nice level ground for camping on. The scenery along the south branch is very attractive. There has been but very few trees chopped and the bush is thus in its primitive state. The canoe glides along the shade of the over-hanging trees, the reflection of which is seen in the water below, making the first canoe ride one long to be remembered. There are also other places of interest in the neighbourhood which will repay the visitor for any extra trouble he may have taken to reach Bracebridge.

# HOTEL ACCOMMODATION.

## BRACEBRIDGE

British Lion and Queen's Hotel.

## GRAVENHURST

Windsor, Albion, Caledonian & Grand Central Hotel.

## PENETANGUISHENE.

Georgian Bay House, A. Arnold, propr.

## BURK'S FALLS

The Burk, Cataract, and Clifton House.

## PARRY SOUND

Belvidere, Sequin, Albion and Thomson House. McKellar, W. Taylor, propr. Star Lake, Craig-Ross-Lea Hotel, M. T. Thomson, propr.

## MAGANETAWAN

Kyles and Carrolls.

## AHMIC HARBOUR

Crosswell House, John Crosswell, prop.

## LAKE MUSKOKA

Beaumaris, E. Prowse, prop. Strawberry Bank. T. W. Wroe, prop. Milford Bay, R Stroud. prop. Muskoka Bay, T. M. Robinson, prop. Point Kaye, J. Hutton, prop. Bala, View House, Thos. Currie, propr. and Board's.

## PORT CARLING

Stratton House, John Fraser, prop. Interlaken House, R. A. Arksey, prop. Vanderburg House, C. W. Vanderburg, prop.

## LAKE ROSSEAU

Ferndale House, R. G. Penson, prop. Cloverport House, M. J. Collins, prop. Oakland Park, J. M. Tobin, prop. Windermere, Windermere House, Thomas Aitkin, proprietor. Fife House, D. Fife, proprietor. Cleveland House, C. J. Minnett, prop. ; Paignton House, J. F. Pain, prop. Maplehurst, Maplehurst Hotel, J. P. Brown, prop. Rosseau, Monteith House, J. Monteith, prop.

## LAKE JOSEPH

Port Sandfield, Prospect House, Enoch Cox, prop. Craigielea, Craigialea House, John C. Walls, prop. Shanty Bay, Stanley House, W. B. Maclean, prop. Hamill's Bay, Mr. Hamill, prop. Port Cockburn, Summit House H. Fraser & Sons, props.

**For terms etc., see advertisements.**

# "GUIDES."

Guides may be engaged from $1.00 to $1.50 per day. Boats and canoes extra. The following are recommended by the Navigation Company:

## PORT COCKBURN:

WM. BRADEY, FRED. BRADEY, BEN. BRADEY, FRANK WING, ROBINSON BROS.

## BEAUMARIS:

ROBERT PHILLIPS, WM. BLACK.

## PENETANGUISHENE:

PAUL VASSIER, JOHN BRESSETTE.

## BRACEBRIDGE:

JOHN COOPER.

## PORT CARLING:

GARRIE JOHNSTON, FRANK FOREMAN, RICH-ARD FOREMAN, FRED PENSON.

## ROSSEAU:

ABRAHAM ASA, THOS. WEBSTER, JOHN PETERS.

## FOR MAGNETAWAN COUNTY:

GEORGE ROSS, SPENCE P.O.; DAN STARRATT, BURK'S FALLS P.O.

## FOR BLACKSTONE AND CRANE LAKES:

ROBINSON BROS., PORT COCKBURN,

# FISH AND GAME LAWS OF ONTARIO.

## FISH.

Bass...................... 15th June to 15th May.
Pickerel and Maskinonge .. 15th May to 15th April
Salmon-trout and Whitefish   1st Dec. to   1st Nov.

The above varieties can be taken in season without obtaining a license or permit.  The season for brook or speckled-trout fishing is from 1st May to 15th Sept. for which a license or permit is required.

## GAME.

Common Deer............. 15th Oct. to 20th Nov.
Woodcock................. 15th Aug. to   1st Jany.
Snipe and Plover......... 1st Sept. to   1st Jany.
Duck and Partridge....... 1st Sept. to   1st Mar.
Swans or Geese........... 1st Sept. to 15th Mar.

All residents outside the Provinces of Ontario and Quebec will have to pay a fee of Ten Dollars per annum for the privilege of deer shooting, and no one person, whether a resident of Ontario, Quebec, or elsewhere, will be allowed to take more than five deer. Two persons hunting together are not to exceed eight deer, and no hunting party to exceed twelve deer.

Penalties are provided for the violation of any of the above regulations.   No eggs of game birds to be taken at any time.

# National Manufacturing Co.

## OF TORONTO.

### MANUFACTURERS OF

## AWNINGS, TENTS, CAMP BEDS, CHAIRS, TARPAULINS, WATER-PROOF SHEETS, FLAGS, WAGGON & HORSE COVERS.

---

**Painted Window Shades, Plain and Decorated.**

---

**TENTS, CAMP FURNITURE AND FLAGS FOR HIRE, CHARGES MODERATE.**

## 70 KING ST. WEST,  -  TORONTO.

# PROSPECT HOUSE,

### PORT SANDFIELD,

**ENOCH COX,** - · - **Proprietor.**

**Terms : $1.75 per day, transient ; $9.00 per week**

**Special Rates for Families for the Season.**

The location of the hotel is unsurpassed, being directly at th
junction of the two Lakes Rosseau and Joseph, and has good
accommodation for 250 guests.   It is the centre of the
best fishing grounds.   It has a fine sandy beach for
bathing.   Its postal and express arrangements are
complete, mails to and from the house daily.

Fine dining-room and an excellent table is set ; and no pains will b
spared in making visitors feel at home.   The Navigation Compan
despatch their fine steamer " Nipissing " from Gravenhurst on th
arrival of the train from Toronto and Hamilton, direct to Por
Sandfield.

# The Stanley House,

Situated in Shanty Bay at the head of
Lake Joseph, Muskoka.

Telegraph Communication, Lawn Tennis and Archery Grounds

**Splendid Bathing for Ladies and Children.   Sandy Beach.**

THE BEST FISHING IS TO BE FOUND AT THE HEAD
OF THIS LAKE.   THE MOST BEAUTIFUL LAKE
AND THE BEST HOTEL IN MUSKOKA.

*W. B. MACLEAN,* - - *Proprietor.*

**POST OFFICE ADDRESS, YOHO.**

## PORT CARLING.

# TOURISTS, CAMPERS & OTHERS

GO TO

# FRED'K D. STUBBS

FOR

## ;ood Fresh GROCERIES, PROVISIONS,

### CANNED GOODS,

CHOICE HAMS, etc., BAKER'S BREAD.

---

A GOOD SUPPLY OF

**)ry Goods, Boots and Shoes, Clothing, Glassware, Crockery, Lamps, Oil, etc., always on hand.**

A GOOD ASSORTMENT OF

---

## SHING TACKLE, CAMPERS' REQUISITES IN TINWARE, &c,

**HARDWARE in various lines and branches.**

---

Confectionery Department replete with the choicest of Candies, Biscuits, etc.

---

### STATIONERY DEPARTMENT

here you can buy the latest Books, NOVELS, Guide Books, Maps, etc. Note Papers, Envelopes, etc.

---

### DRUGGISTS' DEPARTMENT

ntains the most reliable Medicines ; a choice variety of Perfumes, Pomades, Toilet Goods, etc. A good selection of Fancy Indian Work.

---

ICES MODERATE.      Orders by Mail promptly attended to.

7

# INTERLAKEN HOTEL,

## PORT CARLING, MUSKOKA.

Most central house on the Muskoka Lakes. This hotel has been enlarged, remodelled and newly furnished throughout. Tourists will find it a comfortable home.

*Terms Moderate.*  R. A. ARKSEY, Proprietor.

---

## JOS. S. WALLIS,

### *General Merchant,*

Issurer of Marriage Licenses,
Comm'r for taking Affidavits,
Dealer in REAL ESTATE,

### DRY and FANCY GOODS,

#### HARDWARE,

### Boots & Shoes, Groceries,

Machine, Lighting and other Oils.

Timber, Lumber and Shingles,
Planing and Matching
done to order.

*Builders' Supplies a Specialty.*
Steamer "JUBILEE."

Office, Cor. Medora & Maple Streets,
**PORT CARLING, MUSKOKA.**

---

## PORT CARLING

## SUMMER RETREAT,

### CHERRY GROVE.

### Vanderburgh House

Has a dock to itself. Steamers will call daily in July and August, and other seasons of the year on application to Captain. This House, situated on an airy point, will accommodate Forty. It has a good Bathing house, a good quite place for rest, Boating and Fishing and good Tent Grounds. Florence Island for sale with a good house on it, information will be given on application. The steamer "Kate Murray," will be for charter as usual, her wide-known reputation has proved her a success under the management of the proprietor, she will be for sale at the end of August. **Terms from $1.00 per day.** Special rates for families.

**C. W. VANDERBURGH,**
PROPRIETOR.

---

# Strawberry Bank House Summer Resort

## *MUSKOKA LAKE.*

This desirable residence to be let for the summer season. One and a-half miles from Beaumaris, splendid view of the Lake. Good Fishing and Bathing. Boats for hire. M. & N. N. Co.'s Steamers call on signal or by previous arrangement.

*Address:* **T. W. WROE, Beaumaris P.O.**
**Lake frontage Building Lots for sale.**

# Milford Bay House,

## NEAR

## BEAUMARIS.

Beautiful Walks and Drives. Lawn Tennis and Croquet delight the tourist at this resort. Springs of pure water abound, and bathing on a splendid sandy beach perfectly safe for ladies and children. Row Boats may be had also. There is accommodation for about eighty guests at terms from $6.00 per week to $1.25 per day. Steamboat arrangements are excellent.

Mails daily.

*R. STROUD,* - *Proprietor.*

# VIEW HOUSE,

## BALA FALLS,

### MUSKOKA.

The outlet to Georgian Bay of the Muskoka waters.

**Thos. Currie, - Proprietor.**

This comfortable house is pleasantly situated, over-looking the picturesque and romantic Bala Falls, with a fine view of the Muskosh river and Lake Muskoka.

**Has accommodation for Fifty Guests.**

A supply of boats at the house for hire. Good fishing in the immediate vicinity, particularly on Moon River, where Maskinonge are to be caught without a doubt.

# Paignton House,

## JOHN F. PAIN, Prop.

This favorite SUMMER RESORT, delightfully situated on the shore of Lake Rosseau.

*Accommodation for 50 Guests.*

Good Board, also Boating and Fishing, etc. Steamboat Wharf.

Cleveland's Post Office quarter mile distant.

# Beaumaris Hote

## TONDERN ISLAND,

## MUSKOKA LAKE.

---

ACCOMMODATION FOR 150 GUESTS. SITUATIO
SPECIALLY SUITABLE FOR HAY
FEVER PATIENTS.

---

*Good Fishing, Bathing and Boatin*

LAWN TENNIS, BILLIARDS, ETC.

---

TERMS : $1.50 to $2.00 per day.

BOATS FOR HIRE.

---

## HAY FEVER.

---

Beaumaris Hotel, from its elevated posisition, is specially suitable to pe
troubled with this complaint. Read letters on pages 66 and 67
in this Guide Book.

## EDWARD PROWSE,

PROPRIETOR.

# MAPLEHURST HOTEL

## LAKE ROSSEAU.

This beautifully situated summer tourists resort was built in 1886 speciall

with a view for the bette accommodation of the tourist in this romantic and health giving region. It is strictl first-class in all its appoint ments. BOATING, BATH ING, FISHING, LAW TENNIS, BILLIARDS, &c. Post Office in the House. Daily Mail and Telegraph. Mail Steamers call at wharf daily.

**TERMS: $2.00 and $1.50 a day; $12.00 and $10.00 a week.**

**A reduction made in case of large families.**

J. P. BROWN, - Prop. & Manager.

---

## OAKLAND PARK

### HOTEL,

### TOBIN ISLAND,

**Opposite Head of Port Carling River, Lake Rosseau.**

---

**GOOD STEAMBOAT WHARF.**

---

### Terms : from $1.25 per day.

Special Rates for Families.

---

## JOS. M. TOBIN,
PROPRIETOR.

---

## LAKE VIEW HOUSE,

### HUTTON'S BAY.

This Hotel is beautifully situated on Muskoka Lake, 16 miles from Gravenhurst, has some of best fishing points on the Lake. Only half a mile from Brandy Lake. Noted for Bass Fishing. Good Bathing. Daily Mail.

---

RATES: $1.00, $1.25, $1.50, according to rooms. Special arrangements by the week. Capacity of house, 40 to 50 guests. Boats on hire.

**JOHN HUTTON, Proprietor.**

---

Also "Lake View" Cottage to rent, furnished. Apply,

J. HUTTON, Point Kaye, Ont.

# Robinson's Muskoka Bay.

Quiet Private Board in retired locality. TERMS: $1.00 per day, with the use of boats.

T. M. ROBINSON, Box 186, Gravenhurst P.O.

**P.S.—A Yacht to charter for cruzing by the day or week.**

---

## WINDERMERE HOUSE

SITUATED ON THE SHORES OF

### LAKE ROSSEAU, Muskoka, Capacity, One Hundred.

Improvements constantly being made with the view of adding to the comfort and pleasure of its guests. For description of surrounding, see page — of Guide.

### Terms: from $1.25 to $1.50 per day.

**Special Rates for Families.**

### THOS. AITKIN, Proprietor.

The Public Library contains volumes on Philosophy, Mechanics', Science, Art, History, Poetry, Biography and General Literature. The Free Reading-Room will be furnished with draughts, dominoes, periodicals, standard magazines, the Toronto daily newspapers, and one or two of the New York and Chicago dailies. Provision will be made for the giving of Lectures and other Literary Entertainments.

## BOATS

### Tourists and Camping Parties

Supplied with

### Boats, Peterborough Canoes, Tents

At reasonable rates, by day or week. A good supply of boats always kept by the undersigned at the hotels Port Carling, Windermere, Maplehurst and Rosseau. Applications by letter should be sent to Rosseau and will receive prompt attention.

*Oars, Paddles and Oarlocks for sale.*

**Boats put in repair.**

**HENRY DITCHBURN, - Boat Builder**
**ROSSEAU.**

---

**W. J. JOHNSON** Near the docks and bridge are boat houses, where a fleet of skiffs of all sizes nod and dance at anchor. Furnishing boats to tourists in quite an industry here in the summer, quite apart from the numbers used by the residents. Every one rows here as a matter of course, and it would not be very surprising if from these home-trained oarsmen some of the record makers of future races may come.

The resident boat builder here is Mr. W. J. Johnson. His boat house and shops adjoin the locks upon the upper side, and are very convenient to all hotels. He builds a good variety of boats upon light, easy-running models, and of sizes to suit the requirements of all customers. It is needless for tourists coming from a distance, or for a short stay, to encumber themselves with boats, as they can be rented from Mr. Johnson by the trip, day, or week. They can be engaged by mail or ordered by post card from any of the lake hotels, and will be promptly forwarded by steamer to any point desired. Mr. Johnson has just erected a handsome three-storey dwelling, just below the bridge, on the south side of the river, where he may be found when not at the boat house.

Address: W. J. JOHNSON, Port Carling.

# The Belvidere Hotel,

## PARRY SOUND.

This Hotel is open during the Summer Season to receive guests.
The Hotel occupies a beautiful and commanding position
on a height of land overlooking the waters and
numerous islands and channels of Parry Sound.
The air is pure and the scenery beautiful.
The numerous islands and channels are
very picturesque, and afford excellent opportunities for boating,
camping and fishing.

✢ TERMS MODERATE. ✢

## THE PARRY SOUND HOTEL CO.

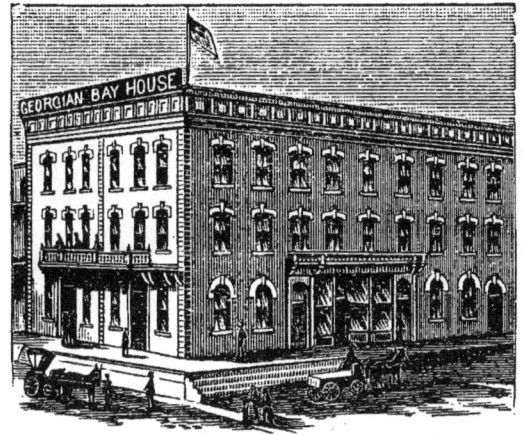

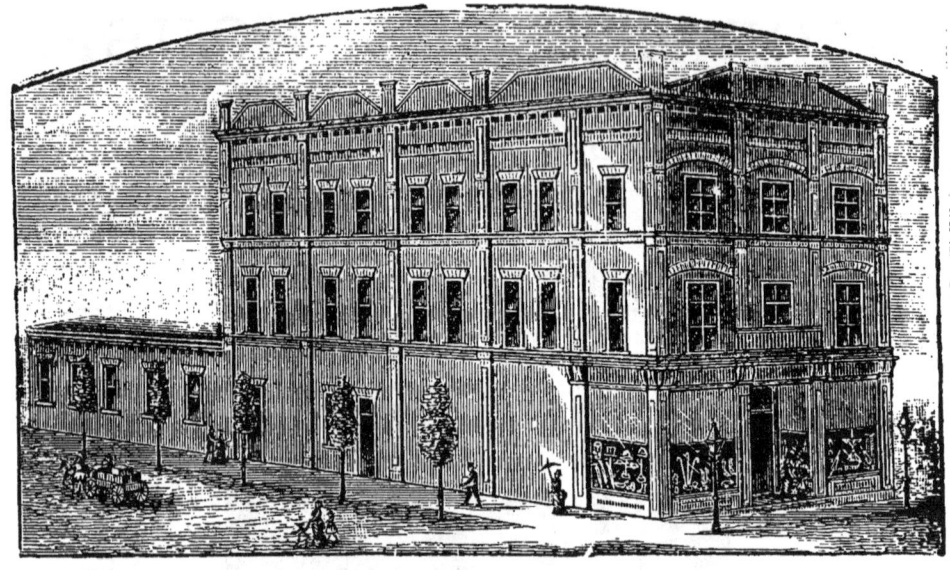

# THE BURK HOUSE,

## NEAR TO THE BURK'S FALLS STATION

)n the Northern and North-Western and **Canadian Pacific Junction Railway,** and north from Toronto about midway between
**Lakes Muskoka & Nipissing,** and being several hundred
feet elevated above **Lake Ontario,** has the pure and
invigorating atmosphere peculiar to the high lands
of the **Muskoka District,** so beneficial to
sufferers by pneumonia, and malarial and
other fevers.

The NEW BURK HOUSE, just completed, is a commodious
ommercial and Summer Hotel, in a bend of the Maganetawan
.iver, and is about 200 feet from and fronting on a charming slope
own to its banks, near the steamboat landing. A 'Bus meets all
ains and steamboats : of the latter the large side-wheel and screw
eamer of the Muskoka and Nipissing Co.'s lines leaves Burk's
alls daily for the foot of **Ah-Mic Lake,** passing down the river and
rough **Se-Sebe Lake.**

The waters of the neighbourhood abound in **Brook and Lake
rout, Bass, Pickerel, etc.**

In its issue of 29th January, 1887, the Toronto *Globe* gave a des-
iption of the route and stations of the Junction Railway, and
itorially said :

"There are few places which are more attractive to the tourist, the
easure seeker, or the searcher after health. The air is pure and
acing, and the scenery in the village and on the way down the river
simply grand. * * * The site (of Burk's Hotel) commands some
the most charming views in the neighbourhood, if not in the whole
trict, and this will render it a most desirable summer resort."

---

*LECTRIC BELLS.*　　　*TELEPHONE CONNECTION.*

## TERMS : $1.50 TO $2.00 PER DAY.

). F. BURK, - Proprietor.

8

# ALBION HOTEL,

## Gravenhurst, Muskoka, Ont.

---

THIS FINE NEW HOTEL IS NOW OPEN
FOR GUESTS.

---

The Apartments are Large and Comfortable,
**CHARGES MODERATE.**

---

The Albion is centrally situated for travellers by both
rail and steamer.

### F. WASLEY, Proprietor.

---

# TOURISTS

WILL ALWAYS FIND A

# GOOD SUPPLY OF READING MATTER

— AND —

## FISHING TACKLE

— AT —

## HUBER'S BOOK & VARIETY STORE,

### BRACEBRIDGE.

# SIGN OF THE "RED FLAG."

**The Oldest Continuous House in Bracebridge.
Established in 1870. Dealer in**

# Dry Goods, Ready-made Clothing,

## HATS & CAPS, BOOTS & SHOES,

## FRESH GROCERIES, ETC.

Tourists and others visiting Bracebridge will find as heretofore, by calling on me, that they will meet with civil treatment and goods they can rely on. My motto has been and shall continue to be "Good Goods at Honest Prices."

Place easily found by looking for "THE RED FLAG." Daily Boat from 3 to 4 hours to do your business.

BRACEBRIDGE, 1888. **J. W. DILL.**

---

## J. L. FENN & CO.
### BRACEBRIDGE,

DEALERS IN

## SHELF AND HEAVY
## *HARDWARE*

Tourists' Goods a Specialty.

### FISHING TACKLE, TENTS,
ETC., ETC.

N.B.—All Goods delivered at wharf free of charge.

### J. L. FENN & CO.

## FRUITS

FOREIGN ✦ AND ✦ DOMESTIC

### *FRUITS!*

All Kinds of Fruits in Season.

### CONFECTIONERY OF EVERY DESCRIPTION.

Orders from Tourists a Specialty,.

## *BALL BROS.,*
### *BRACEBRIDGE.*

# INDEX TO ADVERTISEMENTS.

## OUR OWN HOLIDAY PARADISE.

*Family Man*—NO, DAME FASHION, I'M GOING FOR REST AND RECREATION THIS SUMMER, AND I'VE FOUND OUT WHERE TO GET IT!

# WALKER HOUSE

## *TORONTO, ONT.*

This favourite and commodious HOTEL is conveniently situated to the
principal Railway Stations, Steamboat Landings and Parliament
Buildings. It has ONE HUNDRED and TWENTY-FIVE
WELL-VENTILATED BEDROOMS, besides spacious
Public and Private Dining and Drawing-Rooms. The
house is heated throughout by steam, giving a comfortable temperature during the coldest weather;
and its fine site, overlooking Toronto Bay
on Lake Ontario, renders it a very
desirable Summer resort.

---

TERMS :—$2.00 and $2.50 per day, which includes room and
attendance, with Full Board (Table d'Hote) from a Bill of Fare
comprising the best that the market affords.

*Passenger Elevator. Also Telegraph and Telephone Connections.*

---

The Transfer Hotel Omnibus and Luggage Waggon, and the "Walker
House" Porter attend the arrivals of all Passenger Trains and Steamboats.

### D. WALKER, Proprietor.

# COPIES OF THIS GUIDE CAN BE HAD

—BY WRITING—

## J. A. LINK,

Sec'y. Muskoka Navigation Co.,

Enclosing 10c. in stamps.                    GRAVENHURST, Ont.

CPSIA information can be obtained
at www.ICGtesting.com
Printed in the USA
LVHW08s0610210818
587618LV00019B/500/P